M000014727

The Monopoly of Man

INSUBORDINATIONS / ITALIAN RADICAL THOUGHT
Lorenzo Chiesa, series editor

The Monopoly of Man

Anna Kuliscioff

translated by Lorenzo Chiesa
with an introduction by Jamila M. H. Mascat

The MIT Press / Cambridge, Massachusetts / London, England

© 2021 Massachusetts Institute of Technology

All rights reserved. No part of this book may be reproduced in any form
by any electronic or mechanical means (including photocopying, recording, or
information storage and retrieval) without permission in writing from
the publisher.

This book was set in Arnhem Pro and Bebas Neue Pro by The MIT Press. Printed
and bound in the United States of America.

Library of Congress Cataloging-in-Publication Data

Names: Kuliscioff, Anna, 1854–1925, author. | Mascat, Jamila M. H., writer of
    introduction. | Chiesa, Lorenzo, translator.
Title: The monopoly of man / Anna Kuliscioff ; introduction by Jamila Mascat ;
    translated by Lorenzo Chiesa.
Other titles: Il monopolio dell'uomo. English
Description: Cambridge, Massachusetts : The MIT Press, [2021] | Series:
    Insubordinations: Italian radical thought
Identifiers: LCCN 2020011239 | ISBN 9780262045391 (hardcover)
Subjects: LCSH: Women—Social conditions. | Women—Economic conditions. |
    Women's rights. | Women in the professions. | Socialist feminism.
Classification: LCC HQ1236 .K85 2021 | DDC 305.4—dc23
LC record available at https://lccn.loc.gov/2020011239

10 9 8 7 6 5 4 3 2 1

Contents

Series Foreword

Insubordinations are creative and innovative double negations. They occur when an existing negative condition, the state of being "sub" or "under" a given order and thereby having an inferior rank, is countered by negating this very subjection. In our current late-capitalist predicament such a reversal acquires a more complex meaning. The ordering authority is in fact no longer simply in crisis and exposed to resistance but profoundly disordered in its own operative structure. Today, powers traditionally devoted to regulation perpetuate and reinforce their effectiveness by continuously deregulating themselves. Orders become more and more oppressive precisely as they unveil the inconsistency on which they rest. As Pier Paolo Pasolini presciently put it almost fifty years ago, by now, "nothing is more anarchic than power." In this desolate scenario, actual insubordination cannot but arise as the tentative search for a new kind of order. Its long-term and admittedly ambitious mission is the establishment of a society without subordinates, called "communism." Its first and more realistic task is a taxonomic critique of an Order that resolves itself into myriad conflicting, yet no less tyrannical, suborders.

The present series aims to dissect the contemporary variant of the double negation involved in insubordination through the privileged prism of Italian radical thought. Starting from the late 1970s, Italy emerged as a laboratory for test-piloting the administration of the state of exception we are now living on a planetary level, both geopolitically and in our everyday lives. A brutal repression put an abrupt end to an intense season of social and political emancipations. But the theoretical elaboration of that defeat, which should not be confused with a grieving process, has managed to promote Italian radical thought to the center of a series of international debates that endeavor to define a new function and field of revolutionary politics. The series moves from the assumption that while so-called Italian Theory remains a vague and awkward category and attempts at hegemonizing it run the risk of resurrecting the idea of a national philosophy, it is beyond doubt that a growing number of left-wing Italian authors have, for good reasons, become very popular worldwide.

Drawing on philosophy, political theory, psychoanalysis, architecture, art history, anthropology, sociology, economics, and other fields, this interdisciplinary series intends to both further investigate consolidated Italian theories of emancipation and introduce authors (both present and past) who still remain largely unknown among Anglophone readers. Insubordinations: Italian Radical Thought will also foster original critical

readings that pinpoint the tensions inherent to the oeu-
vre of prominent progressive thinkers and develop novel
dialogues with various strands of post–World War II mili-
tant thought (such as heterodox Marxism, biopolitical
theory, feminism of difference, social psychoanalysis,
antipsychiatry, and theories of fascism). The series will
also translate works by seminal earlier Italian authors
who may be regarded as "forerunners" or critics *avant la
lettre* of current trends in Italian radical thought.

It is my hope that, by delving into the titles of this
series, readers will be able to appreciate the disciplined
indiscipline they all share.

Lorenzo Chiesa

Introduction: Portrait of a Socialist Lady

Jamila M. H. Mascat

A Revolutionary Reformist: Kuliscioff and the Birth of Italian Socialism

"In Milan there is only one man, who is actually a woman," wrote Antonio Labriola in an 1893 letter to Friedrich Engels, reporting on the "state of the art" of Italian socialism.[1] The woman was Anna Kuliscioff, one of the founding members of the Socialist Party of Italian Workers, whose cosmopolitan militancy in Russia, Switzerland, France, Great Britain, and Italy at the turn of the twentieth century actively contributed to the flourishing of the Socialist International and, above all, to the construction and "deprovincialization" of Italian socialism.[2]

Born Anja Rozenstein to a wealthy family of Jewish merchants in Simferopol (Crimea) around 1854, Kuliscioff left Russia in 1871 to enroll in the Polytechnic of Zurich, where she was initiated in the exact sciences and also took philosophy classes. Influenced by nihilism like most of the educated Russian youth of her generation, Kuliscioff sharpened her rebellious temper in the Bakunian circles of anarchist students in Switzerland. In 1873 she married the young Russian anarchist Piotr Makarevic, with whom she moved to Odessa following a tsarist decree that forced all students abroad to return to Russia. Together they joined in the fight against the despotic regime of Alexander II as members of the populist group of the Čajkovcy (Circle of Tchaikovsky). A year later Makarevic was arrested and sent to Siberia, while Kuliscioff managed to reach Kiev, where she lived underground and joined the Buntari, an insurgent organization inspired by Bakunian ideas that was working to spark a peasants' revolution in the region. After a bench warrant was issued against her for instigating sedition in 1877, Kuliscioff fled Russia and reached Lugano. There she finally changed her last name from Rozenstein to Kuliscioff, as a tribute to coolie workers (*Kuli* in German).

Back in Switzerland, she became acquainted with such major representatives of European socialism as August Bebel, Jules Guesde, and Wilhelm Liebknecht, and established friendships with revolutionary compatriots such as Georgi Plekhanov, Lev Deutsch, Pavel Axelrod, and Vera Zasulich, who in 1883 founded Emancipation of Labour, the first Russian Marxist group.

In 1877, during an international congress at Saint-Imier, near Bern, Kuliscioff met the Italian anarchist exile Andrea Costa, with whom she began a passionate and stormy love story marked by frequent arrests and imprisonments—Kuliscioff herself was jailed three times between 1877 and 1879, in Paris, Florence, and Milan.[3] In spite of long and recurrent forced separations, Costa and Kuliscioff evolved together politically, sharing a growing disillusionment with their early insurrectionist convictions and progressively embracing reformist party strategies. While their political partnership shared a firm common ground, their love was troubled by irreconcilable differences in personality, and especially by Costa's jealousy and his aversion to Kuliscioff's emancipated ways.[4]

In 1882, soon after giving birth to their daughter Andreina, Kuliscioff left Imola, the Italian town where she had lived in Costa's house since the previous year, and returned to Bern, where she took up the study of medicine. The irreversible crisis in the relationship with Costa coincided with considerable hardship: Kuliscioff was pursuing her medical studies between the universities of Naples and Pavia while caring for her daughter alone, on a very small income and suffering from the tuberculosis she had contracted while imprisoned in Florence in 1878. Despite these arduous circumstances, in 1886 she finally became the first woman in Italy to graduate from the Faculty of Medicine at the University of Naples, with a thesis on the bacterial origin of puerperal fever. About two years later, having trained as an obstetrician and gynecologist between Turin and Padua, Kuliscioff started her practice at a charity clinic in Milan, where she became known as *la dottora dei poveri* ("the poor people's doctor"). Unfortunately, worsening health conditions forced her to give up her profession in 1895. From that point on, she devoted her life entirely to politics.

With Filippo Turati, the Milanese lawyer who became her lifelong partner after they met in Naples in 1885, Kuliscioff shared a strong commitment to the building of Italian socialism, not without frequent political disagreements. Their apartment near the Duomo in Milan became home to gatherings of socialist workers, intellectuals, and party members and functioned as the newsroom of *Critica Sociale*, the journal they founded in 1891, which they romantically referred to as "their little daughter" in their correspondence.[5] Although she had no institutional position in the newborn organization, renamed Partito Socialista Italiano (PSI) in 1895, Kuliscioff was unanimously recognized as one of its most eminent and influential leading figures, who fiercely opposed anarchist tendencies within the party and contributed to shaping its reformist program, which she viewed as the most advanced strategy for the workers' movement at that juncture. Yet, in spite of her well-known reformist leanings, police authorities had Kuliscioff on record as a subversive agitator who "did not miss any chance to instill the masses with class hatred." This was the picture of her given by the local government office of Milan when she was arrested again in 1898, after the food riots in May of that year, of which she and Turati were accused of being among the instigators; the same record also highlighted her "relentless propaganda" and its wide-ranging impact on the working class.[6]

A representative of the PSI's moderate majority, who would always criticize the "futility of intransigence,"[7] Kuliscioff positioned herself against the Jacobin and maximalist tendencies of the party and backed Turati's "minimal programme," consisting of partial reforms that the socialists wanted to see implemented in exchange for supporting liberal governments. In line with this strategy, Kuliscioff was asked by the party to draft a bill for a new labor legislation designed to protect women and children workers against long hours and conditions endangering their health and safety.[8] The bill for the protection of women and children's rights was presented to parliament in 1901 by Turati and finally served as the base for the 1902 act known as "Legge Carcano" and for the social measures later approved by the centrist executive of Giovanni Giolitti.[9]

For the next two decades, until her death in 1925, Kuliscioff's public militancy revolved around the "woman question," campaigning both for universal suffrage (within the Socialist Party, but often against the prejudice of many of her fellow comrades) and for the organization of proletarian women and the improvement of their working conditions—an issue at odds with the opinions of the most prominent Italian feminists, who saw the defense of women workers' rights as a serious threat to their access to the labor market. Her relentless campaign for women's right to vote on the one hand, and her fight for the liberation of proletarian women from the yoke of patriarchy and capitalism on the other, made her a controversial figure both in feminist and social-ist circles, where her voice struggled to gain consensus. However, by her tireless efforts, she finally managed to convince her party to support women's suffrage and pro-pose a substantial amendment to the new electoral law awaiting parliamentary validation—a law that had origi-nally aimed merely to extend the right to vote to illiterate men above the age of thirty. In spite of the PSI's and Turati's personal defense of universal suffrage, the bill finally approved in 1912 maintained restricted suffrage, allowing only men to the ballot box and excluding mi-nors, criminals, the mentally ill, and women. This was a bitter defeat for Kuliscioff: "By now," she commented, "any Italian who finally wants to be a citizen has only one precaution to take: to be born male."[10] Nevertheless, together with her fellow socialist feminists, she believed it was necessary to give renewed strength to the combat, and engaged in propaganda via the columns of the *De-fense of Women Workers* (*La difesa delle lavoratrici*), the newly founded bimonthly journal of the Labor Organi-zation of Socialist Women, which she codirected until

1914 and which eventually ceased publication in 1925, the year of her death.

After supporting Italian participation in World War I and gradually pushing Turati from his initial neutralist convictions to agreeing with her own interventionist position, in the aftermath of the war Kuliscioff faced the sudden emergence of fascism, the ejection of Turati's reformist wing from the Socialist Party in 1922, and the accession of Benito Mussolini, a former socialist, as prime minister after the fascist March on Rome. The whirling catastrophe in which the country was embroiled threw her into a state of despair. Before passing away, she confessed in her last words that in those days "even dying has become such hard work."[11]

Anna Kuliscioff died on December 27, 1925. Her funeral at the Monumental Cemetery in Milan was attended by a huge crowd gathered to pay their last homage to the "lady" of Italian socialism. Emblematically, the ceremony was disrupted by a sudden attack from a group of fascist Blackshirts.

A Socialist Feminist: Kuliscioff and the Woman Question

A libertarian opponent of marriage (which she considered to be one of the "two currently predominant forms of the servitude of women," the other being prostitution), the mother of Andrea Costa's natural daughter, and the companion of Filippo Turati in a free relationship that lasted more than three decades, Kuliscioff conducted her life in defiance of the dominant morals of her age.[12] Her feminist stance on equality between the sexes resonated with her own experience as an emancipated and educated woman who finally gained entry into male-dominated territories like medicine and politics, just as her claims in defense of women workers reflected her socialist commitment to the class struggle.

The nihilist movement that emerged in the late 1850s right after the defeat of the Russian Empire in the Crimean war influenced Kuliscioff's early formation and shaped her rebellious attitude against privilege and prejudice. As she recalls in her unpublished 1880 essay "Nihilism," "The [Russian] youth, looking at the punishments [inflicted by the nobles on the peasants], felt an instinctive hatred against everything that incarnated despotism and its consequence, the omnipresence of slavery." Family, traditional morality, and education were considered the most blatant incarnations of the tyranny of the tsarist regime. This is why, in her words, "the first steps toward emancipation began at home, where young daughters tried to liberate themselves from paternal despotism, and young women from their husbands'. In other words, visions of new relationships within the family emerged everywhere." As Kuliscioff remarks, the revolts initiated in the household did not simply target socially established "ideas, feelings and habits," but also their "outward manifestations," such as, in the case of women, "the pettiness of feminine vanity": "So as to avoid having to deal with their appearance, women cut their hair, wore short dresses, and took on a rather masculine look; wanting to get rid of their absurd school education, young people conceived of free thinking in the widest sense, and even denied any intellectual authority outside their own reason and inquisitiveness."[13]

Besides the early libertarian imprint of nihilism, the later immersion into anarchist and socialist milieus nurtured Kuliscioff's political consciousness and brought her to associate the "woman question" with the "social question." Socialist convictions shaped and oriented Kuliscioff's feminist views, and rapidly distanced her from the liberal feminist circles that she encountered in Milan, in particular the Lega promotrice degli interessi femminili founded in 1879 by outspoken feminist journalist Anna Maria Mozzoni, the translator of John Stuart Mill's *On the Subjection of Women* and a key figure of Italian suffragism. In spite of Mozzoni's rapprochement with the socialists during the 1880s and her participation in the Lega Socialista Milanese founded in 1889 by Turati and Kuliscioff, the polemical duel between the two feminists, sparked by Kuliscioff's proposal of a labor legislation for the protection of women and children in the late 1890s, mirrored the divergences between the two main orientations of Italian feminism at the time: on the one hand, a majoritarian independent feminist stance that focused on the defense of women's rights (and especially women's right to vote), considering "women" as a universal subject beyond class divides; and, on the other hand, Kuliscioff's isolated "socialist feminism" that viewed the oppression of women through the lens of class interests and class struggle, foregrounding the combat of the "feminine proletariat."[14]

However, it would be unfair to reduce Kuliscioff's feminism to a—so to speak—monistic class inclination. In fact, Kuliscioff always provided a twofold understanding of the woman question, and consistently developed a twofold strategy for women's liberation within the workers' movement and against its patriarchal structures. In Kuliscioff's view, since woman "is not only a slave to the capitalist, but also a slave to her man," women's battle is doubled: on the one hand, women have to fight alongside men against capitalism; on the other hand, they have "an immediate struggle to sustain which is different from the one fought by men" and addresses them as a target.[15]

Being strongly persuaded that "an economically dependent woman will always have a master" and never be free, Kuliscioff set as a cornerstone of her feminist vision the necessity for women to achieve economic emancipation from their male partners and their families as a premise for liberation.[16] The emancipation of woman, therefore, primarily consists in her becoming "an autonomous person who has a right to work and to live working," and labor thus constitutes a fundamental ground of feminist struggles—most importantly, one that also reveals the exploitative relationships at play even among women.[17] In this respect, Kuliscioff opposed "the confused conception that considered the women's movement as a matter of sex, as an indistinct mass."[18] Accordingly, she rejected the universalistic discourses of bourgeois feminists and their elitist defense of the interests of upper-class, privileged representatives of womanhood. As she remarked, if "for bourgeois women, men and exploiters are synonymous, for working class women, the exploiter can also be a woman."[19] Kuliscioff thus deemed "sentimental and utopian" a feminist struggle that ignored social divisions and concealed the conflicting interests of women opposed to one another across class divisions.[20]

In fact, her strategy resulted from the "double consciousness" of the oppression of women by patriarchy and the exploitation of women at work by both male and female capitalists. Contrasting the intolerable living conditions of proletarian women with the ease and comfort enjoyed by women of the upper classes, Kuliscioff claimed that the socialist and feminist causes should not be conflated. No doubt, liberal and socialist women may share common goals; yet while "socialism and the emancipation of women are connected issues that permeate each other, and the triumph of the former cannot be separated from the latter," she maintains that socialism and feminism can only be "parallel social currents" that "will never make one cause."[21]

Speaking anachronistically, one could say that Kuliscioff's approach is based on a "unitary theory" that understands capitalism and patriarchy as intrinsically interlocked rather than viewing them as two autonomous systems.[22] However, in practice, Kuliscioff's "unitary theory" translates into a dual strategy of militancy premised on the fact that the complicit unity of the structures of patriarchal oppression and capitalist exploitation does not simplify resistance but rather increases the complexities of its multiple fronts.

Both at home and at work, gender inequality affects all women, from the lawyer to the rice-weeder (an emblematic figure of the rural feminine proletariat of Northern Italy). Yet, despite sharing a common condition of discrimination, women at different levels of the social scale experience sex disparity with varying severity. Similarly, freedom does not mean the same thing for proletarian and bourgeois women, although moral and social restrictions rigorously apply to both. The workload of domestic labor weighs on the shoulders of poor women workers much more heavily than it does on the shoulders of their wealthy employers. In other words, if the woman question cannot be unilaterally reduced to the proletarian women question, so the interests of privileged women cannot be identified with the interests of all women as such.

Amidst this web of asymmetrical and conflicting relations, Kuliscioff chose to invest her feminist engagement in the class-based organization of women as a semiautonomous force within the workers' movement. With this aim, she exhorted women workers to unite and fight in their workplaces. In her 1898 appeal to workers in the tobacco manufacturing industry, Kuliscioff passionately advocated solidarity among women as the only means for the weak to defend themselves, and strike as the only weapon by which they can scare the capitalists. "You are not weaker because you lack force or intelligence," she reminded them; "rather, you are weaker because you lack the weapons for attack and defense." Similarly, addressing the seamstresses of Corso Magenta, Kuliscioff stressed that when women unite, they "become stronger than their bosses."[23]

As a feminist socialist, Kuliscioff constantly invested her energies in facilitating a convergence of feminist struggles with socialist goals. In this respect, for the purpose of strengthening the presence of women within socialist ranks, she contributed to the creation of the Labor Organization of Socialist Women and encouraged women workers to unionize and join the Chambers of Labor (Camere del Lavoro), while working to raise awareness among both proletarian and peasant women of their own power and the need to struggle for better working and living conditions. At the same time, Kuliscioff fought to gain support for the women's cause from her fellow socialist comrades and to integrate classical feminist claims for juridical equality and universal suffrage in the socialist agenda, harking back to the 1891 Erfurt Programme of the German SPD (Social Democratic Party).[24] For Kuliscioff, indeed, the defense of women's rights must be part and parcel of the socialist program: since women represent a huge (and growing) portion of the working class, their condition should matter significantly to the socialists.

Kuliscioff's dual feminist struggle, against bourgeois feminists in the name of women's labor rights, and within the Italian Socialist Party against the widespread sexist reflexes of its members, in the name of sex equality and universal suffrage, triggered recurrent polemics and remained controversial: on the one hand, feminist circles criticized her strong commitment to the socialist cause, on the other, fellow socialists often remained skeptical about her arguments against the discrimination of women.

After her death, Kuliscioff's legacy was hagiographically appropriated by the Italian Socialist Party or fully inscribed by interpreters in the history of the PSI.[25] The limited fortune of her feminist thought and practice, however, testifies to the scarce interest shown to her contribution to the history of twentieth-century feminism by later generations of Italian feminists, who have tended to view her all-encompassing socialist commitment as ultimately detrimental to her feminist engagement.[26]

Undoubtedly, Kuliscioff identified socialism as the main horizon of women's emancipation, and placed class struggle in a crucial position within the woman question. However, for her, socialism was not merely an economic solution to the evils of the world, but a "moral solution" that would transform humanity into the "consortium of the free and equal." Woman "belongs to socialism" as "a worker, as a mother, as a woman": thus women cannot desert the socialist fight, since if half of the army is missing, the war is most likely to be lost.[27] Hence her vigorous appeal for women to join the Party: "Oh comrades, you outcasts, you forgotten, eternal victims, rise up! Oh slaves, be citizens! Oh females, learn to be women!"[28]

Labor, Suffrage, and Freedom: Kuliscioff's Feminist Writings

The majority of Kuliscioff's writings appeared in *Critica Sociale*, the journal she founded with Turati; in the PSI's daily, *Avanti!*; and in the bimonthly *La difesa delle lavoratrici*, which she also cofounded in 1912 and codirected until 1914. As these were joint intellectual efforts, many of Kuliscioff's articles were signed with the initials "T.K." (Turati-Kuliscioff), or "Noi" (Us) as an index for the couple, or at times with editorial board collective signatures such as "La direzione," "Critica Sociale," or "La difesa delle lavoratrici." A very few texts, including *The Monopoly of Man*, were signed by her name.[29]

As much as Kuliscioff's twofold feminist and socialist militancy, her writings reflect the tensions and contradictions resulting from the distinct fronts of her political engagement. Most of her texts originated as political interventions in current struggles and debates, and therefore adopted manifestly propagandistic and polemic tones, responding to the necessity of opposing prejudice, pleading, convincing, disputing, or infusing strength and courage into the ongoing fights.

Kuliscioff's feminist writings essentially revolve around two major themes: labor and the right to vote. Both issues—women's labor and women's suffrage—were at the center of harsh debates between Kuliscioff and bourgeois feminists on the one hand, and socialists reticent to embrace the cause of women on the other—as manifestly shown by, respectively, her public disputes with Anna Maria Mozzoni and her "family quarrels" with Turati.

In 1898, when Kuliscioff sketched the draft for a new labor legislation for women and children, Mozzoni sent to the editorial board of *Avanti!* (March 7, 1898) an open letter accusing Kuliscioff's proposal of limiting "women's freedom to work" and endangering their chances to enter the labor market by claiming rights that would make them look like undesirable employees for capitalist employers.[30] Kuliscioff's riposte—*In the Name of*

Women's Freedom (March 17, 1898)—countered the my-
opic approach to the woman question that barred Mozzoni from understanding the miserable living conditions
in which most women workers struggled.[31] By brand-
ing a labor bill in defense of women a crime against
women's emancipation, Mozzoni proved she had conflated "women's freedom to be exploited" with "wom-
en's freedom" *tout court*—two issues that for Kuliscioff
were simply antithetical. "As long as she is working 12,
14, 16 hours over 24, earning a salary between 40 cents
and 1.25 liras, a woman worker might become a good
working machine—but she will never be able to gain the
dignity of a woman and a citizen."[32]

While acknowledging that the protection of women
had often been paternalistically invoked by conserva-
tives and the clergy as a justification for strengthening
gender-based division of labor and keeping women at
home, Kuliscioff argued (along the lines of the resolu-
tions she proposed at the 1893 Zurich Congress of the
Socialist International together with comrades such as
Louise Kautsky, Clara Zetkin, and Eleanor Marx) that
women's rights *qua* workers' rights need to be defended
and extended by socialists. Indeed, for Kuliscioff, "wherever the proletarian party is politically represented in
parliament, it must first of all fight for a law to limit the
exploitation of waged women slaves." Such a duty is no
gesture of "chivalrous caring," but a necessary fight to
be taken up by socialists in the name of "proletarians

of both sexes," insofar as the enduring of a "pitiless exploitation of women and children" can only be detrimental to the workers' cause. In fact, if class struggle cannot but benefit women workers, the battles women workers fight for their rights cannot but promote the interests of the subaltern classes.[33] "As long as women remain alone and isolated from the general movement, any hope of improving their position in the present time will be dashed," Kuliscioff claimed, while also stressing that "class struggle will never be effective if those hundreds and thousands of women . . . do not join it."[34]

Thus, for Kuliscioff, Mozzoni's mistake lay in dismissing the power of the alliance between men and women workers in the struggle against their exploiters and in privileging the right to work (or work as such) against workers' rights. Countering Mozzoni, for whom the defense of labor rights may ultimately cause women to lose what they have achieved so far, Kuliscioff argued that women run no risks in fighting for "civilized living conditions," precisely because they cannot lose what they have not yet attained.[35]

The polemic between Kuliscioff and Mozzoni was reignited along similar lines in 1906, when Mozzoni and other feminists, including Maria Montessori, presented a petition to parliament in favor of women's suffrage, restricted to women "who belong to certain categories"—an initiative that Kuliscioff sarcastically denounced as the "comedy" of the "ladies' suffrage."[36]

Viewing women's suffrage and class struggle as inseparable political stakes—"Voting is a defense of labor,
and labor has no sex"—Kuliscioff radically opposed all
proposals favoring a partial extension of suffrage based
on education, a measure that in the end would "supply
with multiple votes the natural enemies of the proletariat" and amount to the "assassination of the political
rights of the working classes."[37] For this reason, Kuliscioff claimed that socialist women could not stand with
bourgeois women who only fight to obtain the same privileges as the men of their class, since "such an emancipation of sex cannot shake, and might in fact reinforce, the
hinges of the present economic society: private property
and class exploitation."[38] Instead, she maintained that
it was possible for socialist women to "march separate
and strike together" with bourgeois suffragists. Nevertheless, for Kuliscioff, "the *indistinct feminist bloc*" was
as much of an absurdity as imagining the suppression
of all parties for the benefit of all classes.[39]

On the other hand, the task of convincing the socialists to support women's suffrage was not an easy mission.
"Il voto alle donne" (1910) collects the public exchanges
between Kuliscioff and Turati about the opportunity
for the party to campaign in favor of universal suffrage.
Turati, who had always been much influenced by Kuliscioff's opinions, shared her views on the principle of
equality between the sexes; but like many other socialists, he tactically favored a gradualist line: unrestricted

men's suffrage first, women's suffrage later; participation of women in administrative elections first, and in political elections later. Indeed, Turati believed that the time was not yet ripe for universal suffrage, thought that a campaign in that direction would damage the battle for expanding men's suffrage to the subaltern classes, and feared the unknown consequences that women's access to the political arena might bring. In other words, Turati did not see the urgency of a demand to which he did not ascribe any "immediate beneficial influence." In contrast, Kuliscioff argued that it was in the highest interest of socialists "not to separate the two sexes in a matter that has nothing to do with the difference between sexes."[40]

By accusing the Socialist Party of "electoral misogyny," Kuliscioff wanted to unmask the fundamental contradictions implicit in Turati's discourse, which cited illiteracy to justify deferring women's suffrage while at the same time championing the right to vote for illiterate men. Similarly, she wrote, "Italian women—999 out of a thousand according to Turati, who must have been counting them all—are absent from politics; and to be absent is to be wrong. Well then—out of 9 million men of age, could you please tell us how many actually take part in political life?"[41] In fact, Kuliscioff acknowledged that in the then-current situation, women, far from representing a political avant-garde, were mostly alien to politics. However, she maintained, that was no reason not to involve or solicit them, and that must precisely be the task of the Socialist Party. Reciprocally, propaganda for universal suffrage in favor of illiterate men and of all women—"twice martyred, both by their misery and by masculine selfishness"—would be, according to Kuliscioff, the only means to "infuse new youth into our party," blighted with "premature old age."[42]

At a time when women were entering the labor market on a massive scale and competing with men in greater numbers, Kuliscioff also saw it as crucial to counter and deactivate the arguments about competition that had become increasingly commonplace even within the workers' movement. It was fundamental to explain that women were not rivals but rather allies of men, and were usually subjected to much worse exploitation. If competition exists, it is the creation of the capitalists who brutally exploit women workers and perpetrate their "slow martyrdom" and "collective murder."[43] "Woman initially offers her work power on the market at a lower price," Kuliscioff wrote, and "the capitalist, of course, is very happy to be able to take advantage of woman's physical needs to push her into the vortex of competition with man's work". Furthermore, she continued, "Woman causes a depreciation of the work of man, who is then by necessity forced to offer his arms at cheaper rates; this in turn brings a decrease in woman's wages, and so both wages fall to the point that they are not even enough to support the family—and then a third element of competition comes onto the scene: the child. So in order to live, the whole family must offer itself to vampire capital."[44]

In Kuliscioff's view, protection of women's labor against long hours, miserable salaries, and irregular and occasional work would be the only way to break the chain of exploitation that intensifies competition among workers and deteriorates their working conditions. In this respect, Kuliscioff argued that any damage caused by the detrimental role accidentally played by women's workforce on the labor market because of its super-exploitability was to be obviated not by excluding women from work, but rather by demanding equal salaries for both sexes.

Kuliscioff's feminist writings display her relentless effort to inscribe the women's cause in the socialist fight for social justice and social emancipation. "Is there a woman question?" she asked. "But if the worker woman is as exploited, oppressed, and equally stripped of capital as the man worker, is it possible then to separate her cause from the great question that agitates the whole modern world, that is, from the social question?"[45] Indeed, Kuliscioff believed that "the woman question is strictly related to the workers' question" and that "like the workers' question, [it] is essentially an economic question." Therefore, the woman question is nothing but "part of the social question, and will not be solved other than with it."[46]

Elsewhere, Kuliscioff explained the historical process of women's liberation by reclaiming once again the crucial function of labor:

Just as it was the great industry that gave rise to the formation of armies of workers who were driven by the force of things to conscious organization of their forces, so also the same great industry will take merit for woman's emancipation. It will almost seem like a heresy. How is it possible? So the industry that snatches woman from the home fires turns her into a competitor to her father and brother, sacrifices her underage children in factories and workshops is to be called the woman's redeemer? Yet, it is so. As long as woman remained locked within the walls of domestic life, performing humble work or, as in more advanced times, working at home on the loom, how could the consciousness of having a social value, of also being creators of social wealth arise in her? Machines, the great revolutionary force of the industries, have also revolutionized woman: first and foremost, emancipating her from the cooking stove and placing her in a condition of struggle for existence equal to that of man; making her equal to man in misery, and in the aspiration to shake the yoke of capitalism.[47]

Labor, in other words, is not only what earns women the right to political citizenship and juridical equality with men but also what "will emancipate [them] in their intimate relationship with the other sex."[48] In spite of her long-standing efforts to claim and establish a substantial link between women's liberation and the construction of socialism, Kuliscioff was perfectly aware that the convergence of the two causes was far from automatic.

Only men could maintain that "the emancipation of the man worker will necessarily also be an improvement in the situation of women," thus mirroring "the same reasoning as the bosses'. Every bourgeois will say: what do the workers want? As long as our business is going well, workers will also be much better off."[49]

Drawing further on the same parallelism, Kuliscioff warned against the risk that "even if an economic revolution took place, [woman] would be considered by the majority of men as an ignoramus, a straw brain; the same as the bourgeoisie did with the working class, after all the revolutions made with the blood of the worker, in the name of freedom and equality—triumphant, it left the worker with the freedom to starve and placed his equality in Paradise."[50] Thus, women should make sure that "if ever the fourth state comes, which is the male proletariat in power, we should not remain in the conditions of the fifth state, without rights of any kind and always full of duties, as it has been up to now."[51] Accordingly, Kuliscioff encouraged women to organize and take their cause into their own hands: she saw it as very unlikely that "a socialist republic, even if it should come soon, would do us the justice we deserve."[52] Therefore, she concluded, "The emancipation of the proletariat can only take place through the work of workers of both sexes. But the emancipation of woman can only take place through the work of woman herself."[53]

The Monopoly of Man

On April 27, 1890, Anna Kuliscioff became the first woman to deliver a talk at the Philological Circle in Milan, whose membership was at the time denied to women. Titled *The Monopoly of Man*, this was her first public speech on a feminist topic: the text, published four years later, can be considered the Italian manifesto on the woman question. The room was full, and Kuliscioff's passionate and radical speech garnered enormous success, apparently pushing a proud Turati to comment that "they should have thrown her out of the window for what she was saying."[54]

A summation of Kuliscioff's feminist strategy, the speech sets out in condensed form the major tenets of her engagement with women's struggles. Drawing on August Bebel's *Die Frau und der Sozialismus* (1879), a seminal work that established the German SPD's line on the matter, *The Monopoly of Man* provides a summary reconstruction of the historical oppression and subaltern condition of women in every society of the past. While denouncing men's multiple and anachronistic privileges "in the family, civil and political rights, and the field of the struggle for existence, both material and intellectual" in modern times, it contrasts the "monopoly of man" with the double exploitation of women, perpetrated by employers and husbands alike, in capitalist society.[55]

In the course of a historical overview depicting woman's evolution "first as a *domestic animal*, subsequently as a *slave* and *servant*, and in the end simply as *subjected*" and a "working machine," Kuliscioff also remarks that the claim for equality between the sexes has often been overlooked by the greatest emancipatory movements in history—from the advent of Christianity to the French Revolution. "Even the French Revolution of 1789, which demolished every institution based on divine right, was not so advantageous for the cause of woman, and, in spite of its great principles of liberty, fraternity, and equality, decided to leave her confined to the role of housewife and denied her civil and political rights. Condorcet and Sieyès vehemently called for her political and social emancipation, but the authoritarian Robespierre and the Jacobins did not listen to them."

Historically, men—no matter what class they belong to—have defended their privilege against women as a natural phenomenon, using religion, science, and morals as their weapons to reaffirm their monopoly. Nevertheless, with the appearance of the workers' movement and the emergence of the socialist cause, the pariahs of society began to protest and demand better living conditions, and women—"the last and most numerous of pariahs who form half of humanity"—also began to rise up. Here Kuliscioff privileges the question of labor, because, she argues, this is "the kernel of the whole woman question, as I firmly believe in the following great and fundamental truth of modern ethics, which is valid for both man and woman: labor alone, of whatever nature, divided and remunerated with equity, is the actual source of the enhancement of the human species." Labor, in other words, makes of women a social value that contributes to the growth of society and, by releasing them from the prison of the household, fosters their emancipation. If "woman worker" is still a "blasphemous word" for many, for Kuliscioff this becomes a "redemptive word," as she firmly believes that "it is precisely modern industrialism, with all its evils, that will make poor women equal to men and will emancipate them from their dependence on the other sex."

In the course of her speech, Kuliscioff describes and reviews the living and working conditions of distinct categories of women—the factory worker, lawyer, teacher, trader, office worker, doctor, and mother, whose peculiar function is analyzed from a rigorous class perspective[56]—so as to show the state of inferiority to which all women are condemned, but devoting special attention to proletarian women, illustrating in detail the significance of "woman's invasion of industries" and its consequences. With the help of facts and figures, Kuliscioff elucidates the actual presence of women in the factories (49.32 percent versus 27.10 percent of men), showing that in some sectors—especially the textile industries—the army of women workers represents a larger portion of the workforce than that of its male counterparts. Thus, she argues, "only when labor is equitably remunerated, or at least remunerated like man's, will woman take the first and most important step forward, since it is only by becoming economically independent that she will withdraw from moral parasitism and conquer her freedom, dignity, and the actual respect of the other sex."

Here, Kuliscioff advances for the first time the principle of "equal pay for equal work," which she considered part and parcel of the claim for social, political, and juridical equality that would be defended in the SPD's Erfurt Programme in 1891 and promoted by the Socialist International. In this respect, Kuliscioff argues extensively against the traditional objections used to undermine such a principle, which was nevertheless "gaining more and more ground in public opinion," and shows to what extent none of the objections proposed actually rely on any objective justifications or factual conditions. On the contrary, she remarks, all objections against wage equality are based merely on the social inferiorization of women, an unnatural and unfounded condition that is in turn perpetuated by unjust wage inequality itself. But history, as Kuliscioff will recall later, breaks this vicious circle and "equates the sexes under the same exploitation by capitalism," making inequality in contemporary society an anachronism. Kuliscioff concludes her speech by stating that "the bottom line is simple": the triumph of the cause of women demands more solidarity and support among them and "less intolerance" from men.

If her commitment to gaining more than halfhearted support from socialist men for the emancipation of women appears beyond doubt, Kuliscioff's dedication to the feminist cause has frequently been questioned in the literature. Clearly, she was cautious with regard to the limits of political alliances among women, theorizing that solidarity, indeed, cannot easily be extended to all feminist groups, but is rather to be premised on their class engagement in defense of proletarian women and the exploited. "Feminist apoliticism"—the faith in the possibility of pursuing women's struggles beyond any party division, and the abstract ideals that moved liberal bourgeois feminism—only aroused her contempt for its supporters' arrogant defense of privileges. Kuliscioff's claim for a selective feminist solidarity appeared controversial, and was probably responsible for the neglect of her figure and her political engagement in favor of women's emancipation within the genealogy of Italian feminism.[57] *The Monopoly of Man*, nevertheless, is considered her best feminist intervention and her greatest contribution to the woman question.[58] Occasionally, feminist scholars have contrasted Kuliscioff's famous speech with her later effort to draft a labor legislation for the protection of women and children, a project that has been interpreted as the beginning of the regression of Kuliscioff's feminist consciousness and its definitive subordination to the "reason of the party."[59] But such a hard and fast judgment seems in many ways unfair and misleading with regard to an understanding of the complex and controversial configuration of Kuliscioff's original feminist perspective and painstaking socialist commitment, which took shape through a genuinely acrobatic political exercise that found its first groundbreaking expression in *The Monopoly of Man.* The delicate and relentless task of combining—without reconciling—the distinct and at times divergent instances of women's emancipation and class struggle that Kuliscioff first developed in this speech remained through all her writings the hallmark of her much underappreciated socialist feminism.

Notes

1. K. Marx and F. Engels, *La corrispondenza di Marx e Engels con italiani (1845–1895)* (Milan: Feltrinelli, 1964), 489.

2. The Italian Socialist Party was founded in 1892 as the Italian Workers' Party and renamed the following year the Socialist Party of Italian Workers. Only in 1895 did it adopt its definitive name Partito Socialista Italiano (PSI). M. Addis Saba, *Anna Kuliscioff: Vita privata e passione politica* (Milan: Mondadori, 1993), 113–114.

3. One of the leading figures of Italian anarchism, Andrea Costa later became the first socialist member of the Italian Parliament. He was elected in 1882 as a representative of the Italian Revolutionary Socialist Party that he had founded the year before. In 1892, his party joined the Italian Workers' Party.

4. A. Kuliscioff, *Io in te cerco la vita: Lettere di una donna innamorata della libertà* (Rome: L'Orma, 2016).

5. M. Casalini, *La signora del socialismo italiano: Vita di Anna Kuliscioff* (Rome: Editori Riuniti University Press, 2013), 98.

6. M. Bigaran, "Rozenstejn, Anja Moiseevna," in *Dizionario Biografico degli Italiani*, vol. 89 (Rome: Istituto Enciclopedia Italiana, 2017).

7. In line with her reformist perspective, Kuliscioff strongly opposed the October Revolution after being galvanized by its first democratic phase. In her correspondence with Turati, she showed all her enthusiasm for the February events that forced the tsar to abdicate. As soon as she was informed of it, on March 16, 1917, she wrote to Turati: "I am having an orgasm since yesterday evening as if I were in Saint Petersburg among the revolutionaries" (P. Pillitteri, *Anna Kuliscioff: Una biografia politica* [Venice: Marsilio, 1986], 447). She also explained that a political revolution "in such great style" was not only going to liberate millions of Russians but it could also promote a democratic turn in the history of Europe (Pillitteri, *Anna Kuliscioff*, 448; see also G. Savant, "La rivoluzione russa e i socialisti italiani nel 1917–18," *Diacronie: Studi di Storia Contemporanea* 32, no. 4, 2017).

8. P. Passaniti, ed., *Lavoro e cittadinanza femminile—Anna Kuliscioff e la prima legge sul lavoro delle donne* (Milan: Franco Angeli, 2016).

9. Kuliscioff's outline of the new labor legislation, as given in her 1897 text "For a Law on Women and Children's Labor" published in *Lotta di classe*, was much more advanced than its subsequent partial implementations. It was largely betrayed by the 1902 "Legge Carcano," which drew only minimally on Kuliscioff's draft even as it purported to integrate its demands (Passaniti, *Lavoro e cittadinanza femminile*, 27). These included: the maximum limit of 48 working hours per week and the right to 42 hours' rest per week for women; a ban on labor for children under the age of 15 and on night shifts for all women and minors under 20; the prohibition to hire women for dangerous and unhealthy jobs; women's right to two months' maternity leave (a month before and a month after giving birth); the maximum limit of 6 to 8 working hours per day for minors between the ages of 15 and 20; regular labor checks by inspectors elected by women workers and paid by the state (A. Kuliscioff, *Scritti* [Milan: Fondazione Anna Kuliscioff, 2015], 109–110). In her 1897 address "To Italian Women" ("Alle donne italiane") in view of the next political elections, Kuliscioff posed the "serious matter" of women's and children's labor as a priority in the socialist program and encouraged women to demand: "1. The eight-hour work day; 2. Equal pay for equal work; 3. Freedom for women to do what they please with their remuneration; 4. Leave from work in the two months before and the two months after giving birth" (*Scritti*, 97).

10. Kuliscioff, *Scritti*, 191.

11. F. Damiani and F. Rodriguez, eds., *Anna Kuliscioff: Immagini, scritti, testimonianze* (Milan: Feltrinelli, 1978), 153.

12. Kuliscioff, *Scritti*, 60.

13. Kuliscioff, 22–23.

14. It is actually quite inappropriate to speak of Kuliscioff's "socialist feminism," since she explicitly rejected this notion and never identified her commitment to the women's cause with the word *feminism*, but rather employed it in a derogatory sense to indicate "bourgeois feminism," which she considered to be radically distant from socialism (*Scritti*, 202; C. LaVigna, *Anna Kuliscioff: From Russian Populism to Italian Socialism* [New York: Garland, 1991]). The choice of the term is deliberate and aims at emphasizing Kuliscioff's relevant contributions to the history of women's emancipation. See also R. Colombo Ascari, "Feminism and Socialism in Anna Kuliscioff's Writings," in *Mothers of Invention: Women, Italian Fascism and Culture* (Minneapolis: University of Minnesota Press, 1995); Addis Saba, *Anna Kuliscioff*, 103; Kuliscioff, *Scritti*, 68–74.

15. Kuliscioff, *Scritti*, 73–74.

16. Kuliscioff, 65.

17. Kuliscioff, 49.

18. Kuliscioff, 177.

19. Kuliscioff, 106.

20. Kuliscioff, 105.

21. Kuliscioff, 107.

22. See Lise Vogel, *Marxism and the Oppression of Women: Toward a Unitary Theory* (Chicago: Haymarket Books, 2013).

23. Kuliscioff, 113, 115.

24. The demand for juridical and political equality between men and women was included in the 1892 charter of the Italian Workers' Party. In her 1892 speech "Feminine Proletariat," Kuliscioff listed four main demands women workers should fight for: "First of all, equal pay for equal work. Divorce. Paternity search. Political and administrative vote" (*Scritti*, 65).

25. P. Pillitteri, *Anna Kuliscioff: Una biografia politica* (Venice: Marsilio, 1986); B. Vigezzi, *Il PSI, le riforme e la rivoluzione: Filippo Turati e Anna Kuliscioff dai fatti del 1898 alla Prima Guerra Mondiale* (Florence: Sansoni, 1981); M. Degl'Innocenti, *L'età delle donne: Saggio su Anna Kuliscioff* (Manduria: Lacaita, 2017), 188–211.

26. Casalini, *La signora del socialismo italiano*, 10; F. Pieroni Bortolotti, "La Kuliscioff e la questione femminile," in Fondazione Giacomo Brodolini, *Anna Kuliscioff e l'età del riformismo* (Milan: Mondo Operaio Edizioni Avanti!, 1978).

27. Kuliscioff, *Scritti*, 99.

28. Kuliscioff, 100.

29. Kuliscioff's intense correspondence deserves a special mention among her writings—especially her letters to Andrea Costa and, above all, her numerous letters to Turati, who moved to Rome in 1896 after being elected as an MP (member of parliament) for the Socialist Party. In the six volumes of her correspondence with Turati (1898–1925), besides the couple's private exchanges, one can also find detailed accounts of Kuliscioff's views about current events, as well as political judgments and analyses that do not necessarily appear in her public interventions (Anna Kuliscioff and F. Turati, *Carteggio*, vols. 1–6 [Turin: Einaudi, 1977]; see also R. Colombo Ascari, "Feminism and Socialism in Anna Kuliscioff's Writings").

30. Damiani and Rodriguez, *Anna Kuliscioff*.

31. Kuliscioff, *Scritti*, 116–119.

32. Kuliscioff, 118.

33. Kuliscioff, 116.

34. Kuliscioff, 72.

35. Kuliscioff, 118.

36. Kuliscioff and Turati, *Carteggio*, vol. 2, book 1, 502.

37. Kuliscioff, *Scritti*, 146, 174, 177.

38. Kuliscioff, 173.

39. Kuliscioff, 174.

40. Kuliscioff, 136, 142.

41. Kuliscioff, 149–150.

42. Kuliscioff, 153.

43. Kuliscioff, 96.

44. Kuliscioff, 9.

45. Kuliscioff, 68.

46. Kuliscioff, 69.

47. Kuliscioff, 63.

48. Kuliscioff, 64.

49. Kuliscioff, 68.

50. Kuliscioff, 74.

51. Kuliscioff, 73.

52. Kuliscioff, 74.

53. Kuliscioff, 74.

54. Addis Saba, *Anna Kuliscioff*, 100.

55. See M. Rebérioux, "La questione femminile nei dibattiti della Seconda Internazionale," in Fondazione Giacomo Brodolini, *Anna Kuliscioff e l'età del riformismo*, 140–154.

56. Interestingly, Kuliscioff suggests that women in the home should earn a salary for doing housework. She writes: "Perhaps housekeepers, who earn a monthly wage for a given work, are financially in a far better position than the wife, who almost never spontaneously receives material remuneration from her better half. Maternity and the management of the household could be a very eminent profession if woman were trained differently for it; if these functions were considered by men-husbands as a profession, superior or at least equal to being a doctor, lawyer, trader, seamstress, and so on; and if one recognized that woman, by the sheer fact of being a mother, already earns for herself material independence, and should receive from the husband a remuneration equal to her work, without having to humiliate herself for expenditures."

57. Addis Saba, *Anna Kuliscioff*, 104.

58. Casalini, *La signora del socialismo italiano*, 106.

59. Casalini, *La signora del socialismo italiano*, 103–122; Bortolotti, "La Kuliscioff e la questione femminile." See also A.-M. Käppeli, "Feminist Scenes," in *A History of Women in the West*, vol. 4: *Emerging Feminism from Revolution to World War* (Cambridge, MA: Harvard University Press, 1983), 482–514.

The Monopoly
of Man

The Woman Question and Other Problems

Ladies and gentlemen,

First of all I must confess that, as I was thinking about the inferiority of the social condition of woman, a question came to mind that left me momentarily perplexed and uncertain. I asked myself, "How can we isolate the woman question from other social problems that originate from injustice and are based on the privilege of sex or class?"

In theory, it may appear that, insofar as any kind of privilege today—as an essential cornerstone of every social institution, all our civil and political rights, and every relationship between the various classes and between man and woman—is everywhere discussed, debated, and losing ground, some small justice for woman—the most affected victim of modern social relationships—should follow suit.

But the experience of many other women who have dared to depart from the traditional paths of female life in general, and especially my own experience, has taught me that, although several generous men, thinkers and scientists—even of the privileged classes—struggle to solve manifold and complex social problems, this is not the case with respect to the problem of man's privilege over woman.

With few exceptions, every man of any social class, owing to an infinity of unflattering reasons for a sex that passes as strong, considers the privilege of his sex as a natural phenomenon and defends it with astonishing tenacity, calling on God, the Church, science, ethics, and existing laws, which are merely the legal sanction of the prevarication of a dominant class and sex. And it is for this reason that, in spite of the intimate connections between these various problems, it seemed to me that I could isolate that of the social condition of woman from all other morbid phenomena of the social organism, mostly generated by that terrible tragedy of life, the struggle for existence.

In this long, continuous, and strenuous struggle, with the progress and development of society, a feeling has germinated that is increasingly self-aware—that of social justice, of civil equality among human beings. Thanks to this feeling, which, unfortunately, is still often unconscious in the proletariat, the worker raises his head and demands labor rights; the peasant, ravaged by ignorance and hardship, not knowing how to consciously claim what he is owed, in spite of perceiving injustice, violently rebels in order to destroy all remnants of feudalism, which are unsustainable in modern social relationships.

All the dispossessed and pariahs of society are on the move; they beg for some light, air, and a life that accords with human dignity. It is therefore only natural that, in our century, a serious and vast movement has emerged among the last and most numerous of pariahs who form half of humanity—that is, women.

Everywhere in Europe and America, armies of women are being built who fight for their redemption and to throw off the age-old yoke imposed on them by the male sex. Although this struggle of women is not very obvious, since—for a number of physiological and psychological reasons—it never assumes that character of harshness and hatred that defines the struggle among different social classes, it nonetheless cannot but involve the tendency to overthrow the privilege of man and shake off his power.

It is for this reason that, intending to speak about the social condition of woman, I have found no better way of coming to the point than highlighting the *monopoly of man* in its various aspects, activities, and social functions.

I know I will face great difficulties dealing with such an issue from this standpoint, since, generally, those who occupy a lower step on the ladder of social coexistence, in order to make themselves accepted, must never assault powerful enemies directly, but may at most modestly ask them for some minor concessions in the guise of a favor and good grace, defend themselves from possible attacks, and never use the ruthless weapon of critique. All in all, they must adjust their voice to humility, if they want to be heard.

However, this is not an indictment. What women demand is not a condemnation of the other sex at any cost; they instead aspire to obtain the conscious and active cooperation of the best men, those who having emancipated themselves, at least in part, from feelings based on habit, prejudices, and especially male selfishness, are already willing to acknowledge the reasons why women must occupy a respectable position in life, since they have attained the right to it.

On the other hand, while denouncing male tyranny, I will have the opportunity to say things about my sex that may in turn seem harsh. But, indeed, I think I am authorized to do so, since I myself belong to it and feel totally sympathetic toward it, even with regard to its weaknesses. Like physical illnesses, the latter cannot be overcome or lessened without first having courageously admitted and diagnosed them. It is beyond doubt that my remarks cannot point at anything absolute; they look for an *average* among things and people, on both sides of which are abundant exceptions that, as is well known, do not at all disprove the rule.

The Condition of Woman throughout History

Those who dispassionately observe modern social phenomena must recognize that the social condition of woman—such an important element of civilization—is one of the saddest phenomena among modern institutions, a residue of an intellectual and moral world that today is disappearing.

A brief talk does not suffice to investigate the very complex causes of this phenomenon, which would require long and in-depth studies and entire volumes. Neither does a more or less brilliant polemic about the inferiority or superiority of woman, or attributing to man's selfishness and prevarication alone her age-old subjection to the other sex, explain a fact that has always been with us, and might have had its biological necessity and historical usefulness, as was also perhaps the case with male slavery.[*]

Whether the origin of the social inferiority of woman was physiological, economical, ethical, or purely the product of the brutal prevalence of force, the fact remains that today's supremacy and privilege of the entire male sex are an anachronism in an age when woman has made progress in every moral and intellectual relation.

---

[*] *Matriarchy*, which was powerful in ancient times and still is among some uncivilized peoples, would seem to disprove that woman has always been subjected to man. But it is to say the least doubtful that matriarchy was and is something more and better than a simple consequence of the necessity to distinguish lineages in clans and tribes that are still sexually promiscuous. That matriarchy did not correspond to any actual moral supremacy of woman over the primitive social group seems to me confirmed by the fact that a greater stability of abodes suffices to make it disappear, without to the best of our knowledge any struggle or reaction by woman, and without any trace or tradition of this supposed ancient authority in the familial forms that immediately followed it.

Although nowadays the intellectual and moral evolution of the human species has mitigated the ancient enslavement of woman and transformed it into a simple submission of one sex to the other, we cannot but be surprised by the fact that, while with the progress of human civilization and culture, since the time of the Stoics and early Christianity, voices were raised on behalf of slaves, the female slave has found nowhere to turn even in Christianity, supposedly the best religion.

On the contrary, if, on the one hand, Christianity sanctified the dignity of woman as the Mother of the Savior, on the other, it served to further consolidate the biblical notion of woman as created from and for man. I would even suggest that never was the contempt for and abuse of woman more manifest and clearly expressed than by the propagators of Christianity. The sayings of Saint Paul, Saint John Chrysostom, Saint Augustine, Saint Ambrose, and others, which all agree in referring to woman as the door to Satan, suffice to prove it. These ideas, subsequently modified and redeveloped by the various Churches, especially the Catholic one, still inform after so many centuries the essence of the opinions men—and, unfortunately, even women themselves—hold about the abilities, attitudes, and reciprocal relationships of the two sexes.

Even the French Revolution of 1789, which demolished every institution based on divine right, was not so advantageous for the cause of woman, and, in spite of its great principles of liberty, fraternity, and equality, decided to leave her confined to the role of housewife and denied her civil and political rights. Condorcet and Sieyès vehemently called for her political and social emancipation, but the authoritarian Robespierre and the Jacobins did not listen to them.

In this way, laws and institutions still exist for women that originated from brute force, were legitimized and sanctioned by the Church, and finally became the basis of existing civil codes.

But in the meantime the cause of women made marked advancement, and, however bound by habits, interests, and selfishness, men themselves had in turn to veil, reduce, and transform their domination.

Yet this is not to say that the subjection of woman is less cruel than it was in the past—also because contemporary woman is no longer the impersonal being lacking individuality and culture she once was. Long gone are the days when woman was regarded as a domestic animal, who could be mistreated, chased away, or killed at her master's whim; or when synods discussed whether woman has a soul, and finally the Synod of Mâcon awarded her one by a handful of votes; or when the founder of the Ursulines gathered theologians in Dijon to decide whether it was a sin to teach woman how to read and write.

Nowadays, almost everywhere in Europe and even more in America, there is no branch of industry in which women do not participate; their primary and professional schools are more and more numerous; they are not denied access to higher education; they are not forbidden the titles necessary to practice all the professions that have so far been, and still are, a monopoly of man. Not even in Italy—which, except for Turkey and Spain, is one of the European countries where the struggle for women's rights has remained in its infancy—not even here is the education of woman now met with the determined oppositions that, until no more than a decade ago, amounted to an almost insuperable obstacle.

Is there a woman scholar in Italy who does not know the persistent and courageous efforts of such intellectually and morally gifted women as Giuseppina Poggiolini, Anna Maria Mozzoni, Laura Mantegazza, Gualberta Beccari, and others, to whom they owe the acquired right of pursuing higher and professional education?

It would therefore seem that, as soon as woman acquires all the necessary qualifications to practice some professions, arts, and crafts, there should be no sufficient reason to subsequently deny her—directly or indirectly—the possibility of practicing them, or to admit her to them on conditions that are far inferior than those of man. And yet, however much this is absurd and unjust, there is a distressing contradiction between the logic of things and their reality.

Woman in the Struggle for Existence

The monopoly of man is too vast for us to treat it here in all its manifestations—in the family, civil and political rights, and the field of the struggle for existence, both material and intellectual.

I will mainly limit myself to the monopoly of man in the field of the struggle for existence, where woman has always played a noteworthy role, which has nonetheless always been subordinated to that of man. Nor could it have been otherwise, when the most effective means to ensure one's livelihood was muscular strength, which is relatively weaker in woman, and when males, driven by sexual instinct, conquered females through the brute force of the physically stronger.

Following Letourneau, we could say that *woman was the first domestic animal of man*, since, given their unequal conditions in the struggle, she was won over by him, but only by brute force. In fact, in the division of labor for the preservation of the species, animated by that powerful force that is maternal feeling, woman showed herself to be active and capable of industrious inventions, even in primitive societies. As Professor Vignoli puts it in his remarkable work on sexual psychology, "in primitive human conditions the protection and care of infants enhance and awaken the mind of the mother and urge her to contrive new forms of industriousness, which are all discovered in the early human age."*

Woman in Primitive Peoples

Woman thus carried out tasks that were equivalent to those of man, or even more strenuous and manifold. Anyone who has read books by explorers and missionaries on the primitive peoples of Africa, Australia, and the islands still inhabited by savages is likely to be shocked by the terrible fate that awaits women. While man's principal occupations are hunting and warfare—which, moreover, are not constant—woman continuously needs to attend to the harshest tasks.

In his *Viaggio nella terra del Fuoco*, after narrating the hard work of the inhabitants of Tierra del Fuego to procure food, Captain Giacomo Bove says that "the major role in this struggle belongs to woman. She carries out the most painful works; fishing, rowing, feeding the fire. . . . How many times did I see men peacefully sitting around the hearth while the poor women were exposed to snow, wind, and rain, fishing for their lazy husbands."

Young Australians ingenuously say that they take a wife so that they can get wood, water, nourishment,

---

*Tito Vignoli, *Note intorno ad una psicologia sessuale* (Milan: Dumolard, 1887), 12.

and have someone carry their packs during the transmigrations of nomadic life. In all the ages of human development, woman's destiny has always been to be considered by man as his working tool.

If we take a quick look at the patriarchal family, woman looks after children and cattle, sews clothes, and builds huts, and, when cultivation began, she was the first animal to be harnessed to a plow.

Because of her usefulness as laborer, and thus not only owing to sexual instinct, man felt it necessary to conquer woman, even in the primitive times of human evolution, first by force—whereby we have marriage through abduction, of which a symbolic tradition remains in the wedding customs of many peoples—and subsequently by means of provision of his labor and bondage. According to the Bible, Jacob worked for seven years in return for Rachel, but her cunning father gave him her sister Leah instead, so as to oblige him to work another seven years, if he wanted Rachel.

Marriage by conquest was followed by marriage by purchase. The groom paid something, almost always heifers, to the owners of the bride—that is, her parents—and subsequently to the bride herself. Perhaps the presents that fiancés still give today when they propose originate from this; although they are no longer regarded as an actual transaction, how many men are unable to find a more effective means to win the heart of a girl than buying her a ring, necklace, or some other trinket that cajoles feminine vanity! However, today—in more civilized times—it does not often happen that man buys a wife, but rather the opposite; that is, it is woman who has to buy a husband. Girls without a dowry know a thing or two about this.

Woman in the Middle Ages

The sad life of slave women in Greece and Rome is too well known for me to recount it. But it would seem that with the beginning of the Middle Ages, under the influence of Christianity—a religion pervaded by compassion and love for one's neighbor—the fate of woman should have improved, since, apparently, woman has always been man's closest neighbor. And yet—forgive my heresy—it was in fact Christianity that sanctioned and, so to speak, legitimized the subjection of woman, which previously had no other foundation than the dominance of the physically stronger. Christian asceticism made men, in their thirst for paradise, consider woman a temptation leading to sin, possible perdition, and, all in all—as I've already said—the gates of Hell.

In this way, the already arduous obligations of woman's work, about which modern housewives have not the faintest idea—since the woman of the Middle Ages had to spin, weave, bleach cloth, manufacture garments and linen, prepare soap and candles, tend the fields, vegetable garden, and cattle-shed, and ultimately see to all the tasks that civilization required to be carried out domestically and which men as warriors disdainfully avoided—were even treated with open contempt, of which she was then turned into a symbol, in the name of a faith that claimed to be humanitarian and redemptive.

How can the nostalgic Romantics speak to us of the poetry of the Middle Ages, its troubadours, castle maidens, and the poetic creations that raised woman to Seventh Heaven?

Were those poetic creations actual women? The Beatrices, Lauras, Leonoras were mere hallucinations, created by the vague intuition of great poets, who felt that man was half a being if not completed by woman; insofar as the real eternal feminine was scorned and insulted, ascetic fantasy had to forge it in the ethereal form of a blonde, lymphatic, and nearly angelical woman, who stood ideally very far away from the poet. These poetic creations do not so much flatter female self-love as sadden the soul, when we realize that, to find an outlet for their affective expansion, ingenious men had to locate the imaginary woman in heaven or in hallucinatory visions. And it could not have been otherwise, given the real condition of woman in those times, when the precepts of a religion that was then in full strength prescribed her obedience and silent suffering as a supreme norm.

Modern Woman

In this way, the entire development of the eternal feminine starting from the primitive ages is presented to us as a long martyrology.

The right of the physically stronger, the principle informing the social organisms that evolved out of the embryonic cell of primitive societies, turns woman into a defeated loser—first as a *domestic animal*, subsequently as a *slave* and *servant*, and in the end simply as *subjected*. This is also why in many families the birth of a female child is regarded almost as a misfortune. Still today, among Bretons in France, in their rustic and imaginative language, peasants say of a woman who gives birth to a baby girl that *elle a fait une fausse couche*.[1] The same phrase is also used in some districts of Russia: they say that woman *sdielala vikidisch'*, that is, she aborted.

However, with the evolution of modern civilization, the element of physical strength was increasingly eliminated from social activities, industrial production, and even agriculture, so that women of the social classes who earn a living through labor gradually found themselves in a situation more or less the same as that of men. And it is especially in our century that, owing to the laws of political economy—which we will not here take into consideration—and by collaborating directly in the production of social wealth, woman could become aware of her equivalence with man.

Current Causes That Drive Woman to Work

The increasingly manifest desire of woman to become economically independent is a specific phenomenon of modern times—since modern life everywhere drives woman to work, out of economic necessity in the great majority of the working and middle classes, and for moral reasons in the small minority of the privileged classes. In fact, even women in the dominant classes are no longer content with being a flower, angel, decorative object, or the docile companion and servant of man, but demand to cooperate with him in social labor and to represent a social value.

Yet, overall, what leads woman to work is the fact that marriage—the only prospect for woman to obtain a relatively secure social position—is itself becoming very difficult; unfortunately, mothers who have girls of marriageable age know this well. How could men welcome the burden of maintaining a family when the struggle for life is getting more and more arduous even for them? And if the girl has no dowry, she is left with nothing but being the laughingstock of a society that calls her a spinster and the bitterness of a miserable and empty life, unless she is prepared to become self-sufficient through her own work.

Moreover, modern life offers unmarried men many of the comforts that, in the past, they could obtain only at home, so that, today, they do not need a housewife to prepare their lunch, laundry and the rest, and thus can avoid the trouble and burden of having a family.

Given the increasing difficulties of life, marriage degenerates into a business deal: the dowry is its objective, the girl an inevitable appendix.

This is so much the case that Germany, England, America, and France hold actual *marriage fairs*, ruled by supply and demand, just like *job fairs*. I am speaking of marriage agencies and publications advertising for those who are after a wife or husband, with their skilled mediators earning a percentage for each marriage they arrange.

And still, in his statistics on weddings, Bertillon speaks of a third of men in France who remain bachelors and, at the same time, numerous marriages between very young girls and honorable men over sixty. With a few exceptions, modern marriage has thus become one of the most shameful selections—a selection of capital, without regard for fondness or great disparity of age. Anthropologists will establish what the advantage of this might be for our species.

In such conditions, it is natural that finding a husband has become one of the most difficult professions. Moreover, if we bear in mind that almost everywhere, except for America, women outnumber men (according to the 1871 census, in England they did so by a margin of almost a million, and by a slightly lower one in France), it is easy to see how, according to Élisée Reclus,

40 percent of women do not marry, and must somehow make a living. Once we include widows, women who separate from their husbands, those who divorce—whose number is increasing enormously in France, Belgium, and Switzerland—we have a whole army of women who, if they did not work, could either sell themselves—and there would be too many—or commit suicide.

It seems to me evident that *it is not only the theoretical idea of emancipation, or any abstract principle, that leads woman to compete with man, but also the struggle for existence in the true sense of the word.*

Why I Chose the Question of Woman's Labor

I have chosen the question of woman's labor because I think it is the kernel of the whole woman question, as I firmly believe in the following great and fundamental truth of modern ethics, which is valid for both man and woman: labor alone, of whatever nature, divided and remunerated with equity, is the actual source of the enhancement of the human species. And, indeed, if every individual belonging to either sex, of the appropriate health and age, perceived the entire moral range of such an ideal and independently obtained their means of subsistence, participating in any way possible in the division of social labor, one of the greatest scourges of modern society would disappear, namely, parasitism—which is so rare among inferior animals of the same species and, unfortunately, so pervasive among the superior animals of the human species.

Giuseppe Sergi—note that I am not quoting an anarchist, or a revolutionary, and not even a socialist, but simply the most celebrated Italian anthropologist—sees in the scourge of social parasitism the most powerful cause of human degeneration. Another sociologist, among the most cultured and studious in Italy—and hence not as well known as he deserves to be—Angelo Vaccaro, shows how "parasitic life harms both the victim and the parasite; the former is subjected to a reduction of vital power, the latter to a reduction of its organic complexity."* When applied to social relationships, this biological law alarms anthropologists and sociologists with regard to the future of the human species, in which parasitism occupies such a considerable position within the great disparity of social classes. But scientists are themselves men, after all, and one would search their writings in vain for an application of such a positive and scientific law to the relationships between man and woman, where it would truly reveal its immense value.

---

*Angelo Vaccaro, *Sulla vita degli animali in relazione alla lotta per l'esistenza* (Milan: Dumolard, 1887), 15.

Woman's Moral Parasitism

I now need to clarify my stance. It might seem strange that having insisted on the fact that woman has always worked—even more than man—I am now labeling her a parasite. But woman's parasitism, and the danger it poses to her and man, is not biological or material, but ethical or moral.

I am not speaking of the very small minority of women who live frivolously, paying visits and spending time at the vanity table, because they are actual parasites and as degenerate as the men of their class. The Roman patrician who tried to vomit repeatedly so as to stuff himself again and again was as degenerate as the Roman matron who, coming home from the circus and having witnessed the agony of the gladiators, entertained herself by torturing her slave women with pins.

But the moral parasitism of the majority of women, on which I would like to focus here, originates instead from servility and submission.

How did the moral selection of woman evolve through submission and servility?

Woman always had to please man in every way. All her intelligence and energy were always aimed at satisfying her master. She had no ideas or feelings that were not those of her ruler.

Woman echoes man, and her personality is almost abolished. If she does not echo him, within the family she must at least pretend to do so, for the sake of keeping the peace; from this follow that shrewdness and proclivity to fiction, which everybody reproaches her with, but which has been her only form of defense, and, if nothing else, a proof of her intellectual power and vitality. If she did not feign and simulate, woman would have been destroyed and reduced to the level of an automaton.

The same happens with children, even good-natured ones, who indeed easily tend to lie only because of their weakness, especially when they have tyrannical parents or guardians. But, fortunately, good-natured children kick this habit and shy away from it as soon as their character reaches a sufficient stage of development; on the other hand, in this regard, women never fully overcome adolescence.

Unfortunately, this state of affairs has not offered woman favorable conditions for the development of her real character.

Character never joins forces with servility.

And, indeed, men and women—especially the latter—who have an independent character are often regarded as rebellious, unsettled and troubled people, a danger to society. It suffices that a woman affirms her personality for women themselves to crucify her, perhaps because this is what pleases man; and, in order to please him, as happens among savages, it is women who abuse their friend, if, for whatever reason and out of misfortune, she falls from the grace of their common master.

It is nonetheless true that the feeling of motherhood has developed in woman the most beautiful and highest aspects of domestic altruism. She is ready to sacrifice herself, with love and resignation, for all members of her family. But these feelings, although they originally stood as the basis of social coexistence, have been in modern times forcedly confined to the restricted circle of exclusively family-oriented interests, and can deteriorate into pettiness and narrow-mindedness. When brought to its limit, family altruism becomes the enemy of social altruism, which woman does not experience much, if at all. As observed by several sociologists, including Professor Vignoli, woman is thereby an essentially reactionary and conservative element of society.

Repercussions for Man

This tendency is not confined to woman. Man himself, in his continuous coexistence with woman, owing to an unperceived and unconscious suggestion, is, willing or not, subjected to woman's full-fledged conservatism, her fear of innovation, and all her antisocial feelings. Like George Dandin,[2] man is being punished for the sin he himself committed. He is the one who wanted such a woman, who keeps and maintains her in this condition; instead of fulfilling man and enhancing his vital power, woman hinders all his enthusiasm, so that he feels like his wings have been clipped.

Perhaps the legend of the biblical hero Samson, whose strength was cut along with his hair by Delilah, contains a primitive intuition of this phenomenon.

Even today, when one needs to tear down the columns of a temple of superstition, strike at the Philistines and annihilate them, undergo a financial sacrifice for some generous purpose, or sacrifice time and effort for something socially useful, for an ideal—which only mildly impairs the family—man bears all the consequences of not having a real companion in his companion, of the fact that woman does not think like he does, concordantly, and does not see how family welfare is inseparable from social welfare.

In these cases, man either gives in or morally distances himself from his wife. In any case, while woman's parasitic life reduces her complexity, because she does not develop intellectually and morally, man in turn undergoes a decrease in vital power, since he must either spend a great part of his most precious energies in sterile fights within the family or sacrifice the best force of his character.

Woman is basically what man made her. Women are not in the least guilty of not having their own ideas and feelings. We would need a league of honest men who, thanks to a more serious and solid education, helped her overcome her eternal minor age—not by means of a medieval knight's courtesies, which only apparently respect woman, but through actual cooperation. This would also be in the interest of man and the human species, since if woman is what man has turned her into so far, vice versa, man is the creation of woman; it is she who influences the development of his character and shapes his intelligence. As they rightly say, while men make laws, women make customs—and we all know that when there is a conflict between laws and customs, customs always have the upper hand.

Nowadays, everybody complains about the decadent character of great and minor men alike. Let woman's character and personality evolve, and you will see woman, the real mother, will raise not cream puffs but real men!

Economic Independence as a Precondition for Civil and Political Rights

It therefore seems to me that only when labor is equitably remunerated, or at least remunerated like man's, will woman take the first and most important step forward, since it is only by becoming economically independent that she will withdraw from moral parasitism and conquer her freedom, dignity, and the actual respect of the other sex. I believe it is only at that point that women will have the moral strength needed not to put up with the pressures of fathers, husbands, and brothers, and will themselves be able to create, among their sex, that powerful weapon of modern social struggles, namely, association, in order to acquire civil and political rights—which are now denied to them, as they are to men interdicted for imbecility, madness, or delinquency.

The existing laws inflict this atrocious humiliation on woman, because not only men but also women themselves consider woman as an eternal minor, and she will be able to come of age only when she will *be sufficient unto herself* through her own intelligence, skills, and moral strengths.

In America, it took half a century of female labor in industry, public education, and the liberal professions (without exception) for American women to obtain not the right to deliberative vote—which was granted in only one of the United States—but the mere right to advisory vote in political bodies, legislative commissions, and general assemblies.

It has only been seven years since the Kentucky General Assembly heard two women, Benet and Hoggart, support the rights of their sex. Naturally, as women who advocate for themselves, they generated great curiosity among both representatives and the vast public that rushed to the House. Skeptical and malignant minds were disarmed and won over by Miss Hoggart's juridical eloquence and erudition; that same day, a bill was presented that awarded women the right to administer their property and, for mothers, an authority over children equal to that of fathers.

This fact—matched by similar cases in France and England, which I am ignoring here for the sake of brevity—

is only an isolated example meant to show how juridical laws are the consequence of social habits and customs, nothing other than the sanctioning of the already existing social relationships, just as cosmic and biological laws are nothing other than the synthesis of observed phenomena.

However, I do not intend to speak in absolute terms, and I will not deny that if today, somehow miraculously, male legislators should grant women civil and political rights, this fact would exercise an immense influence on their intellectual and moral development, since it is a biological law that new functions create, step by step, organs that are adapted to them. Women would experience something similar to the phenomenon we observe in the great mass of male factory workers, who are still not very inclined to civil and political life. And yet, after a few years of the workers' direct participation in political life, we see how formidable orators emerge out of an almost childlike mumbling—orators who have serious ideas about and a profound knowledge of the vital questions upsetting their class.

But, by now, intelligent and sensible people no longer believe in miracles, and the existing laws concerning women will undergo the same evolution every other law has undergone. In the words of Herbert Spencer, I would say that "in proportion as the principle of voluntary cooperation more and more characterizes the social type,

. . . the implied assertion of equality in . . . rights become the fundamental requirement of . . . law."[*]

Hence, by cooperating on an equal footing with man in any aspect of social labor, women will make current laws impossible, laws that put them in a position of inferiority with regard to political rights—among minors and people incapacitated because of imbecility or madness—and assign them such an inferior status within the family with regard to civil rights. However, it is certainly the case that until woman becomes self-sufficient and stops depending on man in order to survive, the law that considers her as a property of the husband—whereby the wife has to follow him wherever he goes—will remain fully in force. And should the legal articles in question, so offensive to woman's human dignity, be abolished, this abolition will remain a dead letter owing to the economic dependence of the great majority of women.

The Privilege of Modern Man

Indeed, men vaguely grasp this entire process of moral consequences that will unfailingly follow as soon as

---

[*]Herbert Spencer, *The Principles of Sociology*, vol. 2 (New York: Appleton, 1897), 536.

women—of not only the lower but also the middle classes—enter the field of the struggle for existence. They create all kind of possible obstacles to prevent the professional work of women.

It is true that man's fear of competition plays a great role in this, which is dissimulated through social ethics arguments, based mostly on religious biases and habit. But by far most influential is the unconscious fear of having one day to renounce, out of love or necessity, the authority and arrogance of his sex, which has been embedded in man since prehistorical times—and I concede that abdicating power is always a difficult and painful thing.

Let us thus consider the modern monopoly of man with respect to the woman who works in industry, education, the arts, and the professions, and assess whether there are sufficient reasons to justify it.

Women Factory Workers

First of all, I will speak of the labor and remuneration of the woman wage worker, since the great majority of women compete with men in the vast field of industrial production, and since, with regard to the comparative moral value of different jobs, it seems to me there is no job about which one should be particularly proud or dispirited; from the point of view of social usefulness, being a seamstress or spinner is not inferior to being a doctor or lawyer.

My approach is also motivated by a question of justice. The woman factory worker is indeed the one who is most affected by the horror of woman's social inferiority. She is doubly enslaved: on the one hand, by her husband, and on the other, by capital.

Adopting a sentimental stance, Jules Michelet exclaims: "The woman worker, what a blasphemous word!" He attributes this phenomenon that appalls him to our iron century. I would rather say: "The woman worker, what a redemptive word!"—since it is precisely modern industrialism, with all its evils, that will make poor women equal to men and will emancipate them from their dependence on the other sex.

The number of women employed in industries and manufacture is a veritable army, which in some countries and specific industries exceeds the army of male workers. Statistics prove this best, although they are uncertain and incomplete since we still do not have actual statistics for labor and wages, and, so far, available data have been provided by private companies and chambers of commerce. They are nonetheless sufficient to give us an approximate idea of the various problems of modern industry.

Woman's Invasion of Industries

Having had an opportunity to research some Italian industries in 1880 thanks to the support of the Ministry of Commerce, Vittorio Ellena found that, out of 382,131 factory workers, 27.10 percent were men and 49.32 percent women, that is to say—leaving aside young boys—103,562 men and 188,486 women, distributed as follows in the various industries:*

	Men	Women
Silk	15,692	120,428
Cotton	15,558	27,309
Wool	12,544	7,765
Linen and Hemp	4,578	5,959
Mixed Weaving	2,185	2,530
Paper	Approximately the same number	Approximately the same number
Tobacco Factories	1,947	13,707
Tanning	All men	

*Vittorio Ellena, "Statistica di alcune industrie italiane," *Annali di Statistica* 13 (1880): 32.

The latter also holds for railroad factories and the rope sector.

If we consider the various regions of the Kingdom of Italy, except for some central regions and almost all the southern regions (where industry is in its infancy), the prevalence of the weaker sex is as follows:

	Men	Women
Piedmont	22,617	40,388
Lombardy	24,438	78,743
Veneto	11,151	21,257
Emilia	4,448	6,114
Marche	2,753	6,248
Tuscany	7,759	11,386

And this does not happen only in Italy.

In 1861, in England and Ireland, 467,261 women were employed in manufacturing as opposed to only 308,273 men. According to Pierre Paul Leroy-Beaulieu, the number of woman workers increased 60 percent over ten years.[*] In fact, fourteen years later, the 1875 census reports that, in England, the number of women employed

---

[*]Pierre Paul Leroy-Beaulieu, *Le travail des femmes au dix-neuvième siècle* (Paris: Charpentier, 1887), 28–29.

in the textile industry alone had already reached 541,837, while that of men was only 233,537.[*]

I could have gathered many similar numbers about England, France, and other countries, but that would have unbearably annoyed the reader. Yet they all confirm this twofold peculiar phenomenon: on the one hand, women's invasion of manual labor, to such an extent that they by themselves form a working class; on the other, the fact that the increase of women in industries is, comparatively, much faster and greater than that of men. It could almost be said that, while for men this increase follows an arithmetical ratio, or one slightly higher than that, for women it follows a ratio than is slightly lower than a geometrical one.

In many industries where men far outnumbered women, the ratio was completely reversed.

For instance, this was the case in England, with the production of raw materials. In 1861, there were around 300,000 women and almost 500,000 men in this sector. In only seven years, the numbers were inverted, and this is a conservative estimate.

---

[*]August Bebel, *Die Frau und der Sozialismus* (Zurich–Hottingen: Verlag der Volksbuchhandlung, 1879), 86.

There are also many industries where the ratio of women to men is three to one—for instance, in the production of so-called *articles de Paris*.[*]

Others are almost completely in the hands of women—such as the processing of pearls and diamonds, and some factories producing musical or surgical instruments, which require a great deal of patience and subtle skills.

In France, the great Gobelins Manufactory and the national printing house employ only women and, judging from their reports, they are very satisfied.

With the improvements to machine design, there are by now very few industries in which women do not participate.

The so-called harmful and dangerous industries are no exception. Suffice it to say that women work in mines in the processing of metals and in factories where noxious chemical fumes cause chronic poisoning.

With regard to women working in factories, who represent the great majority of the female sex, nobody speaks of the family that is at stake, when they have to work ten or twelve hours a day, if not fourteen or sixteen in some sectors. Here femininity, maternity, and the upbringing of children are being trampled on—everything that

---

[*]Edward Watherston, *State of Labor in Europe*, abridged by Mister Viali, *Annali di statistica* 12 (1880).

bourgeois men use to defend themselves when women of their class become competitors in their professions.

The Wages of Women

How is woman remunerated as the producer of so many different goods in every European country?

To answer this question it is again useful to refer to numbers. Suffice it to say that we can infer with reasonable certainty the following conclusion from all statistics (although there are not many): for *equal work*, women are always paid *far less* than men.

As an example, I mention some data offered by the Directorate-General for Italian Statistics in 1882.[*]

Here in the Milan province, at the Cantoni cotton mill, male spinners receive 1.86 liras, female spinners 1; male weavers receive 2.35 liras, female weavers 1.18.

Men who spin flax and hemp are paid 3.20 liras, women 1.05. This ratio is more or less constant in every industry. For equal work, women are always paid one-third to one-half what men earn.

---

[*]"Contribuzione per una statistica delle mercedi," *Annali di Statistica* 14 (1885).

According to Leroy-Beaulieu, in France, men earn twice what women earn.[*] According to Charles Elliott, in Germany, they earn 3 francs to women's 1.60.[†]

We thus understand how it is indeed the case that, when women workers have to make a living from their labor alone, they generally cannot provide for themselves.

And we also understand why so many economists—such as Leroy-Beaulieu and Jules Simon—philanthropic ladies, and Anglican pastors who specifically focused on this issue have all come roughly to the same conclusion Michelet drew in his humanitarian investigation *Le peuple*: "Woman, less pitied, is, perhaps, even more to be pitied. She is in double bondage: though a slave to work, she earns so little with her hands, that the wretched creature must also earn with her youth [to grab something from the pleasures she offers to the other sex]."[‡]

Supposed Causes of Lower Wages: Supply and Demand

What then is the cause of these lower wages for women?

---

[*]Leroy-Beaulieu, *Le travail des femmes au dix-neuvième siècle*, 132.

[†]Charles W. Elliott, "Woman's Work and Woman's Wages," *North American Review*, August 1882.

[‡]Jules Michelet, *The People* (London: Longman, 1846), 38.

Political economy claims that the most general cause that determines wages is the law of competition, that is, *supply and demand*, since human labor is itself a commodity, which is sold on the market like every commodity.

And yet, following this criterion, one could explain why women's wages are so low compared with men's, if indeed nowadays there were an excess supply of female labor.

But we have seen that today women are admitted to industries in numbers similar to male workers, and even more so.

We therefore need to look for another cause.

Lower Productivity

Some will say: lower productive force.

Well, this could be a cause for lower wages if we still lived in a time when physical force were one of the prevalent factors of production.

But today this is no longer the case.

Apart from some very limited spheres—such as porterage and barging—today machines have replaced muscles.

Today, a good factory worker is not required to have an athletic build but to be continuously on the watch and pay attention, be skillful, patient, and dexterous, all qualities that nobody will doubt woman possesses, indeed often to a greater degree than her competitor.

In the county of York, where the wool industry is prevalent—which in the past required great physical strength—there used to be the following saying: "Processing wool requires a man's hand." Nowadays it has been reversed.

Leroy-Beaulieu heard a major industrialist saying that there are many women who simultaneously attend to two or three looms, and not a single man who is able to do the same.

Where people are paid for their output, the wife and daughters of a family often earn more than the father and sons.

We should also consider that, in sectors that employ only women, the workday is far longer.

Judging from a report Senator Paris submitted to the French Senate in 1881, it seems that, in France, the length of the workday for women is on average fifteen and a half hours.

And you all know how long the workday of our silk-weavers and rice-workers is.

It is therefore not woman's lower productivity that can explain her lower wages.

Fewer Needs

Second, they will claim women have fewer needs.

But who determines these needs?

First of all, needs are not constant in quantity. Those who live on water and polenta—with all the horrors of pellagra—certainly have fewer needs than, for instance, a Parisian factory worker who eats meat and drinks wine every day.

After all, woman has to buy clothes and pay the rent, light, and laundry bills, just as man does.

There remains the difference concerning nourishment. But, if woman carries out tasks that are the same as those of man, she will then spend the same amount of energy—and even more, since she is weaker—and hence she should eat more than man, not less.

In this regard, her salary should be higher or at least equal.

The Actual Causes: Division and Deference

Having rebutted these two main objections, advanced by both economists and non-economists to justify the shameful exploitation of female labor, I will now hint at other causes, which seem to me to amount to the actual source of such a huge injustice.

Women are not at all united; they do not resist exploitative capital, and only very rarely use the fearsome weapon of strikes.

Woman defers to tradition, and is more scrupulous than man before authorities; she is ruled entirely by routine and is also more ignorant. According to the most recent census, here in Italy, 73.51 percent of women are illiterate, as opposed to 61.03 percent of men[*]— although it is certainly the case that, with regard to illiteracy, the stronger sex is itself not so much stronger than the weaker.

Given all these feminine virtues—obedience, a less vivid awareness of one's personality, resignation, patience (women have far too much of it!)—capitalists prefer the woman factory worker, since, as a tool that can be better exploited than man, she identifies more easily with the productive machine, and becomes herself a *working machine*.

As I have already pointed out, centuries of servility and submission to male authority have not enabled woman to develop a real character that amounts to the potentialities of acting and reacting.

A Complementary Wage

Finally, they will tell me that woman's wage is lower because it need only complement man's wage.

This seems also to be the opinion of the economists, since one would search in their voluminous works in vain for a word on or mention of women's wages.

---

[*]Luigi Bodio, *Relazione sul censimento generale del 1881*, May 1884, session 26.

They speak of the family wage, of how man cannot earn less than a certain amount of money if he is to support his wife and children. But nobody speaks of the working wife, as if she were an exceptional phenomenon, unworthy of being taken into consideration.

All in all, woman is thus considered a *supplement of man*, and not as an autonomous person who has a right to work and to earn a living.

The Law of Custom

What thereby mainly determines the lower payment of woman is not so much a strictly and properly economical law as this set of concepts and traditions, which I would refer to as the *law of custom*. This is the same law that also contributes to not raising men's wages—albeit less significantly. In this way, especially in agricultural countries, some wages have been kept at the same level since the Middle Ages, in spite of all the vicissitudes of modern progress. For example, this is the case in Tuscany with the infamous *du' paoli* (approximately one lira) that, since time immemorial, is paid to hired hands as a daily payment, which nobody dares to contest—independently of whether crops are good or bad, and of the mercilessness of hail and tax collectors. Now, it is this law of custom that, since the dawn of time, has sanctioned male privilege; it is this relentless law that weighs on the inequity of woman's remuneration.

Women Teachers

The other most accessible career to woman is in education, where she is less contested.

Woman teaches not only in kindergartens, primary schools, and professional schools, but also in fields leading to the highest levels of science—as is the case in America.

In the state of New York, there are 19,400 female instructors as opposed to 8,000 male instructors. Monsieur Hippeau, who was in charge of a French cultural mission to America, tells of women who translate Xenophon and explain geometry. More or less the same holds in other American states. Thanks to a wonderful transformation in America, the system of public education has little by little been almost entirely transferred to the hands of women, who for so many centuries had been kept away from science.

Some very recent data (1889) tell us that the number of teachers in France is 100,000, where approximately half of them are women.

I do not have precise data for the rest of Europe. But I know for a fact that, in Russia, primary education and all-girl high schools are almost entirely in the hands of women.

It seems that even in Italy the number of women teaching in schools and kindergartens is increasing every year, much more rapidly than the number of schools, which greatly alarms the parents of daughters competing for a position.

The Wages of Women Teachers

How are women teachers remunerated?

You will understand correctly that, with equal duties, they nonetheless have fewer rights than men.

Suffice it to say that, in America, a male teacher earns 3,000 dollars, a female teacher 1,900—more than a third less.

And this is America, where, since childhood, girls study on the same bench as boys, where woman, with her activities, has already conquered for herself an incontrovertible place everywhere in society, where women are more respected and also fewer in number than men.

Just imagine how much less women teachers are remunerated in our old Europe!

And yet they secure positions through examinations, and are also favored over their male counterparts; reports are packed with commendations addressed to teaching women.

As happens with the factory worker, here too the actual cause of all this lies in custom: man has the privilege of being male; woman has the misfortune of wearing skirts.

Saleswomen and Retailers

Our remarks become even more mournful when we cast an even superficial glance at the countless army of women employed in trade, as workers in the clothing industry or as accountants.

The poor life of the shop assistant (charged with selling products) has already been abundantly illustrated by literature and statistics. We have extremely eloquent statistics, relative to Paris and London, about the miserable earnings of these wretched girls, who, in addition to carrying out a wide-ranging job, are obliged—like male shop assistants, and even more so than them, who are paid double—to make a *good impression*, as they say, that is, to look well-dressed and smart. This is itself a requirement of the job, not to mention the other times when they are also expected to look pretty.

Think about how these unfortunate girls make ends meet; once sick days and public holidays are subtracted, their salary hardly reaches 600 liras a year!

If added to the husband's earnings, this sum can make life more comfortable in the family. But, for a woman who lives alone, whether a girl or widow, and must provide for herself, think how much effort and sacrifice such limited finances impose upon her.

And if the woman in question must also provide for a child, then we witness true misery, resorting to the Congregation of Charity, prostitution, or unheard of suffering.

The worst part is that the state seems to be encouraging the private sector to pursue the unjust, obnoxious, and shameful exploitation of woman.

Women employed in telegraph and telephone companies, the railways, and the manufacture of tobacco are indeed all regularly remunerated less than men, while they carry out equal functions with equal skills and abilities.

It would almost seem as if labor were sexed, and transformed itself for the sheer fact that a woman is involved.

Is it perhaps that women retailers do not run all the risks and difficulties of trading, like men do? Do they pay lower taxes? Do they have less responsibility when they go bankrupt?

And yet they have no voice in the chambers of commerce.

And when, in France, during the penultimate parliamentary term, there was a public bill about enabling women traders to elect their own judges in the commercial courts, guess who Minister Tirard turned to for advice?

The chambers of commerce, that is, the men who are their members!

This consultation is really quite comical. One might as well ask the pope his opinion on the rights of freethinkers.

We do not need to specify what the answer was and how the bill foundered.

But why should Monsieur Tirard care about listening to women traders about the appropriateness of the fact that, when they have conflicts with their rivals, their interests are in the hands of judges elected by the latter?

After all, this will surprise no one, if we bear in mind that governments always and everywhere defend monopolies and privileges, and the monopoly of male traders should be no exception.

Women Professionals

Having said all this, one should admit that such a state of affairs is beginning to be questioned in the most civilized countries. The principle *Equal pay for equal work* is gaining more and more ground in public opinion.

In France, it was recently proposed to raise the wages of women employed in post and telegraph offices. In Denmark, the government itself is proposing making wages equal. In London, Brussels, and Paris there are now job fairs for women, aimed at defending female labor.

The fact that women have acquired the right to be elected—and, in some cases, have been elected—in departmental and even higher councils for education, as happened recently in France, Sweden, and Norway, is not just a sign of the times but also a guarantee that some justice will soon be brought to the work of teachers.

To date, we cannot say the same of women in so-called liberal professions—that is, women doctors, lawyers, and those who have a degree in the sciences or humanities.

Here bourgeois man is a twofold monopolist—as a male and as belonging to the dominant class—and does everything possible to ruin his rival.

He resorts to so many ploys and quibbles; he invokes intellectual difference (to the detriment of woman, of course), frivolousness and vanity, which would not allow her to apply herself to serious intellectual work with perseverance and dedication; above all, he raises cries of alarm about the destruction of the family, the loss of femininity and grace—you name it!

Starting with pastors and priests, and including scientists such as Bischoff, Waldeyer, and Charcot, they all join forces to contain the invasion of bourgeois women in the intellectual field of the struggle for existence.

Objections

Let us now consider whether there is any truth to these objections.

With regard to intellectual differences, which modern physiologists and psychologists could really rely on data based on brain size? Who doesn't know that the size of the brain varies even among greatly distinguished men? For instance, Cuvier's brain weighed

1,861 grams, while Haussmann's only 1,226, the average size of a woman's brain.

Who ignores the fact that tiny animals, such as bees and ants, which have a minuscule brain mass, are intellectually superior to goats and heifers? And what do we really know about, for instance, the very subtle structure of the brain? Even if a microscope were to provide us with extremely small histological differences between the brains of man and woman, we would still need to consider so many extramicroscopic coefficients, such as molecular composition, the molecular movement of nerve tissues, cerebral chemistry, that no actual scientist would be able to condemn in good faith the weaker sex for its alleged intellectual weakness.

But, even when they do study, what have women discovered? What inventions have they contributed to the scientific capital of humanity?—They believe they can undermine and dishearten us with this sort of question.

But how could one expect women, who have not been studying for long, to become like Newton and Copernicus? In fact, what they have achieved in such a short time is truly amazing.

Moreover, like every other organ, the brain is able to develop. I am prepared to concede that, today, the average brain of woman might be inferior to that of man, since it is the organ she has so far used the least. Although they have a subtler and weaker musculature than men, we saw women participating as a team of firefighters in the Paris exposition, and they did not give in to men in terms of either strength or dexterity. Their muscles must have developed similarly to those of men.

Indeed, Buchner found that in countries where women are not far beyond men in terms of intellectual development—such as England, France, and Sweden—the differences in brain size between the two sexes are minimal. The difference is especially minimal in France.

This is certainly not due to the fact that Frenchmen have lost their minds; this would fully contradict modern history, which, over the last century, presents France as the beacon of modern civilization.

After all, the issue at stake is by now so outmoded and far from serious that I do not intend to bore you any longer with what has been said about it in different guises; I will limit myself to referring to Paul Topinard, a disciple of Broca (the founder of the anthropological school), who expresses himself as follows: "There is no sexual difference with respect to cerebral development, and, considering what comparative anatomy regards as the actual progress in the morphology of the encephalon, we could even claim that in terms of cerebral evolution woman is more advanced than man."*

The other objections are even less worth refuting.

---

*Paul Topinard, *Revue d'Anthropologie*, July 15, 1882, 409.

Female frivolousness and vanity: don't they find a match in the male sex? I do not see any great difference between the female desire for dressing up in feathers, ribbons, and some frills and the urge many bourgeois men have to obtain a cross, insignia, or some other kind of artificial decoration!

We would lose grace and femininity: if these two words dissimulate ignorance, I have to agree that grace is indeed lost. But why should a beautiful and delicate young lady lose beauty if one of the greatest beauties, namely thought, shines in her eyes?

Men also say that an educated woman becomes so pedantic, pretentious, and arrogant—a "bluestocking."

I admit that, at times, especially among the early women students, some are pedantic, precisely because studying is still not widespread among women. Yet in the case of bourgeois women who have long been intellectually equal to bourgeois men, higher education does not make them more proud than knowing how to read and write. American young ladies are the most adorable, and the Russian ones preserve all their simplicity, whether despite of or thanks to their studies.

But I do not want to dwell any longer on objections I deem far from serious; as for the alleged destruction of the family, I will treat it later.

Furthermore, as already stated, the point at issue is not woman's superiority or inferiority; on this ground, many talented women have already engaged in disputes showing an incredible verve. Is there anything left to add to what Jenny d'Héricourt brilliantly wrote in her *Femme affranchie*, where she responds to Proudhon, a stubborn accuser of the female sex?[*]

Everything changes with time; today's republicans and monarchists are different from those of 1848; the arguments in favor of woman have themselves changed in nature.

Polemical debates in this field are now outdated. Even if we were to refer to the infinite number of women who have distinguished themselves on thrones as well as in the sciences and literature, we would still get nowhere. They will protest that the likes of Mary Somerville, George Sand, and Queen Elizabeth are exceptions; but I myself prefer to speak of the great masses of invisible women, rather than of those whose superior ingenuity nobody denies.

I do not even intend to compare the sexes, because I cannot admit that man is the ideal being of creation and should be taken as a measure of comparison. The fact is that woman is neither superior nor inferior; she is what she is; and, such as she is, with all her differences

---

[*]Jenny d'Héricourt, *A Woman's Philosophy of Woman, or Woman Affranchised* (New York: Carleton, 1864).

from the other sex, there is no reason for her to be found inferior.

Do we perhaps have special laws for men depending on whether they are ingenious, mediocre, or idiotic? The same should hold for woman before man, independently of whether she is more or less cultivated, intelligent, and more or less above or below the male average.

Women Physicians

Life itself proves that all the objections by which bourgeois men attempt to close the doors of liberal professions to women fail to block their path.

In America, there are already 3,000 women physicians who work in hospitals and universities, and direct clinics and nursing homes. In the state of New York, ongoing protests are aimed at approving a particular bill that makes it compulsory to appoint women physicians as directors of female asylums. Of 38 states, 33 are in favor of this and only 5 against. In female asylums, more than 20 women physicians have already taken office.

In Russia, more than 600 women physicians are practicing at the moment. They are doctors in hospitals, assistants in scientific laboratories, and medical officers; they widely practice in private with women and children, and chair medical societies, for example in Moscow. After a fierce struggle against their rivals, men physicians ended up accepting the fait accompli; it is possible to crush one, two, or three pioneers but not hundreds of them. There is strength in numbers and petty vicious stratagems no longer suffice to fight them.

Only ten years ago, in Edinburgh, male students expelled the first young women who courageously decided to attend medical school. In today's England, in such a short time, women physicians are highly regarded by the general public. There are already 73 female physicians.

Last year, a women's hospital, directed only by women, opened in London. Women doctors have triumphed. And now, in every main English, Scottish, and Irish city, there are special medical schools intended exclusively for young ladies.

Currently, more than half of the 478 students enrolled in the Boston Faculty of Medicine are women.

In Paris, women physicians are already so numerous that they had to be admitted in competitions for positions as public assistants. Despite what men physicians did to prevent women's access to internships in hospitals, having won those competitions, Miss Melle Klumph and Miss Blanche Edwards were finally admitted as residents, that is, as assistant doctors who can have a career in a hospital.

In 1890, in Paris, eleven women were appointed as external assistant doctors, and not one as a resident, since the examiners, who were all men, preferred male doctors, in spite of the fact that women might be of equal merit.

The University of Geneva enrolls almost 100 female students, and last year the Davy scientific award was assigned to Miss Stefanovskaja, a student in natural science.

Seeing that in certain countries, such as America and Russia, women have so rapidly managed to stand up to men physicians, it would seem one could conclude that their path to medical practice was plain and simple.

And yet the first women doctors can tell us how much and how severely they were obstructed by their male colleagues. How many efforts, struggles, and even tears—I would say without fear of ridiculing myself—women had to endure in order to start a career that is so useful to society!

I have already mentioned that, in Edinburgh, male students expelled female students. In London, pastors delivered sermons from their pulpits claiming that women physicians will initiate the Reign of Satan on Earth. In Russia, the current empress herself did not want women to become doctors. Hospital committees were closing their doors everywhere. And the public had no faith in female skills.

Depending on the person, place, and time, health boards invented all kind of pretexts to reject women physicians. Precisely this was the case here in Milan, when three years ago a woman physician reported to our city's main hospital. She was immediately ostracized. And why? Out of compliance with accepted principles of morality, it seems.

All in all, the early women physicians were heroic in their unequal battle against biases and especially their colleagues; given that they won, we must recognize that the weaker sex showed itself to be stronger than the stronger sex in terms of activity and determination (after everything I said earlier, I very much hope nobody will accuse me of flattering my sex). By now woman has earned a license of competence.

Women Lawyers

The winner is always right. People will say: "I'm fine with women physicians." But women lawyers will make them turn up their noses in contempt.

The Boards of the Bar Association and the highest judicial authorities will prevent women from practicing law as long as there are only a few of them around. When they become legion in Europe, like women physicians, nobody will dare any longer to deny woman her vested right, since she has herself regularly trained and obtained a degree, like every lawyer of the other sex.

Lidia Poët in Turin and Marie Popelin in Brussels were rejected on the laughable pretexts of pregnancy, breastfeeding, and the fact that the lawyer's cap does not lend itself to women's hairstyles and the gown does not accommodate the bustle (now that the latter has become unfashionable, how will they object?). These pretexts do not even manage to dissimulate their vacuity and very much reveal the trickery and efforts used to defend the monopoly of the male caste.

Women Scholars

And what about women scholars?

In their case, to confront the monopoly of man, they at least need to disguise themselves as males as much as possible and sell their merchandise, even when excellent, under the label of a male pseudonym.

The Mother

Now they will ask me: "And the mother? You have spoken at great length about women factory workers, teachers, traders, and professionals, but you forgot women who are mothers."

No, I have not forgotten them; I saved them for last precisely because they are the most important.

While woman's labor specifically concerns the interests of the individual, maternity embraces the interests of the human species, the interests and future of humankind.

We should nonetheless point out that, owing to various physiological and social reasons, maternity is denied to very many women throughout their lives. Others, although they enjoy (or suffer) physical maternity, do not know how to educate their children, and, in modern civilization, the latter activity has itself become a special vocation, like any vocation that leads to a profession or art. In any case, the active time of maternity and the education of children is only a short period of one's life. Even without confining ourselves to bourgeois society—where practical Malthusianism almost always limits the number of children to two or three at most—it is certain that, in general, by the age of forty—when, for both male and female professionals, life and careers are blooming and still amenable to great progress—the function of women who are only mothers is over. They cross their arms across their chest and, so to speak, outlive themselves, feeling useless and a burden to themselves and others. How many women have I met, not of the worst kind and even those who are least relieved by frivolous gossip and idleness, who once they have reached that age consider life to be a great disappointment, cry secretly because of the void they feel inside and around them, and beg for the liberation of death?

Certainly, all this will undergo profound and as yet indeterminable changes when the evolution of family, which is rapidly advancing and dissolving the ancient domestic relationships based on male rule and isolated hearths (as suggested by the continuous increase in the number of divorces, separations, and nonmarital cohabitations), will produce a more elevated form of family founded on spontaneity and equality. It is quite possible that at that point a great part of child protection will be devolved to the community and that a more pronounced separation between motherhood and education will be established, on the basis of the division of labor and the separation of duties, which are typical of the modern age, and are at the same time the cause and effect of all civil progress.

But I do not want to get ahead of my time and will limit myself to considering the condition of women as mothers in the current period of transition.

When she believes that, through marriage, she has reached her goal in life and secured a social position, woman is the being we should commiserate with the most. By losing her surname she also loses her personality. Her life remains fully absorbed by her husband and companion in the struggle for existence. She is master of neither her properties nor her children.

The inferior position of woman in the family can be compensated by the affection and psychic harmony of two beings united by an indissoluble bond and, fortunately, these unions are not unknown. But in most cases, marriage initiates for woman the purgatory of an existence made of long and humiliating suffering.

As I have already said, in most cases, marriage is an investment; rich men marry a dowry and poor men take a wife in order to have a servant. Very few think of the prospect of children or deem it to be a misfortune; they are not at all prepared for the duties and responsibilities of educating children properly.

And what happens when children are born?

Mothers are only "half-mothers." In high society, nannies are hired, because the lady must preserve her beauty, pay and host visits, attend theaters and *soirées*—the child is a nuisance and gets sent to the most remote corner of the home. In the working bourgeoisie, the wife helps her husband by working, and the infant is sent to the countryside with a nanny. In the proletariat, the poor conditions of life force the mother, even in this case, to send the child away, because women must themselves contribute some earnings to their miserable household.

Oh, well, maternity could be one of woman's noblest duties in social life, one that would most satisfy her psychic tendencies and most suit the physical development of her body.

But are the education and teaching of women really aimed at preparing them to carry out the greatest of their duties?

In every class of society, girls ignore everything, and are misguided by the ignorance and prejudices of older women and godmothers.

What do girls know about how babies are born, grow up, and develop? What kind of physiological and hygienic notions are they given that would help them have some idea of how to raise a physically and morally healthy child?

Because women are kept in ignorance, the mother soon loses every kind of moral authority over her children. By the time a boy attends high school, he knows much more than his mother, and what is the result?

The mother's moral harmony and intellectual union with her children diminishes more and more; she is respected, but the son is a branch that detaches itself from the tree, and the mother, after a sad life afflicted by suffering and grief, does not even retain the intimate friendship of her children.

If woman met her duties as mother, shaping the intelligence and fortitude of her children, then her inferiority to the father within the family would itself wane and perhaps fully disappear, since the husband himself—the father of her children—would hold her in esteem and show her respect, which today is so rare. The husband sees in his wife a person he supports, a sheer *ménagère* in the bourgeoisie, a luxury item in high society, and a housekeeper in the poorer classes.

The mission of the wife and mother is so little appreciated as work involving great effort and responsibility that woman has to endure extreme difficulty just to secure a monthly sum from her husband for daily expenses and the running of the household. Not to mention her own personal expenses. The seamstress's bill in many families is a *casus belli* between husband and wife, since the husband does not even acknowledge her right to buy clothes, although he gets angry if she does not make a good impression.

The woman who, as mother and mistress of the house, should have one of the most welcome professions, ends up being considered by the husband as the laziest person on earth—and she is not even given the right to share, with equal authority, the livelihood he earns outside the home. Perhaps housekeepers, who earn a monthly wage for a given work, are financially in a far better position than the wife, who almost never spontaneously receives material remuneration from her better half.

Maternity and the management of the household could be a very eminent profession if woman were trained differently for it; if these functions were considered by men-husbands as a profession, superior or at least equal to being a doctor, lawyer, trader, seamstress, and so on; and if one recognized that woman, by the sheer fact of being a mother, already earns for herself material independence, and should receive from the husband a remuneration equal to her work, without having to humiliate herself for expenditures.

Hopes and Vows

I here come to my conclusion.

The bottom line is simple.

For the triumph of the cause of my sex, I hope only that men will be slightly less intolerant and women slightly more supportive of each other.

Perhaps, at that point, the prophecy of the greatest poet of our century, Victor Hugo, will be realized: he predicted of woman what William Ewart Gladstone predicted of the factory worker—that the nineteenth century would be the "Century of the Woman."

After almost four years, as I am in the process of reprinting this conference, held on April 27, 1890, I have nothing to add except that the numbers relating to woman's presence in every job, art, and profession have all increased considerably; some have even doubled.

Milan, January 1894
A.K.

Translator's Notes

1. *Faire une fausse couche*: "having a miscarriage."

2. *George Dandin ou le mari confondu* is a comedy by Molière.